Our scoliosis stories

compiled by Tia Deacon

Cover designed by Robert Southworth

Dear Reader,

My name is Tia. I thought I'd create this book to not only spread awareness about scoliosis and how common it is, but also to show other people's stories and how their experiences are different.

Some accounts will be longer than others. Although a few contributors wished to remain anonymous, all are written in their own words, and all gave permission for their stories to be included in this book. I'm grateful to each one of them for their contributions.

Mercedes

It was 1986 and I was 13 years old and suddenly started getting back pain. At first my mum brushed it off as 'growing pains', but when I continued to complain, she took a look and realised that my spine wasn't straight. Looking back at school photographs from the previous couple of years, I can clearly see that my shoulders were not straight, so my spine must have been curving without anyone really noticing for quite some time. My GP told me it was scoliosis straight away and referred me to an orthopaedic specialist in London. I got an appointment very quickly and went to the Royal National Orthopaedic Clinic on Great Portland Street in London. I remember thinking how exciting it was to be travelling on the train with my mum to London, as we never did that sort of thing usually.

The building was very old and the room was a huge expanse, but deadly quiet. I remember sitting there in fear of it all; of the unknown. This was no typical hospital, it felt more like a library. I was summoned by a very stern-looking nurse to a row of curtained changing rooms and instructed to remove all my clothes, except for my pants, and put in a hospital gown. Having never done this before, I had no idea what I was doing and remember getting hot and flustered with the whole affair. I had to put my clothes in a shopping basket, which just felt so strange, who does that!? I don't recall where my mum was at this point, she must have been sat waiting for me. Maybe she thought I was confident enough to get on with this by myself, but I really wasn't, even if I told her that. I was taken for a series of x-rays and photographs and even an image of my facial structure was taken. The rooms were cold and bare and very little conversation was had.

Looking back, I wonder why the nurses weren't more considerate, given my young age. It certainly didn't feel like a caring environment, it was all very serious, which just compounded my fears. I eventually stood in front of a number of doctors and nurses who were positioned around a large consulting room. They could see me from all angles and instructed me to turn and bend in various ways for their examinations. I couldn't have felt more vulnerable standing there in just a pair of pants; my emerging adolescent body entirely exposed to these strangers - and my mum! So embarrassing! I didn't really care what my back looked like at that point, I just wanted it to be over as quickly as possible.

Shortly after this appointment, I was sent to another hospital in London to have a dye injected into my bloodstream to check for any issues with my bones. I believe this was done because usually scoliosis isn't a painful condition, yet I was experiencing pain. My dad took me to this appointment and I remember the injection being very painful. We had to wait a couple of hours for the dye to take effect, so my dad thought it would be nice for us to walk around the British Museum for a while, as it was close by. Not long after going in I started to feel very weak and faint. I had to sit down and my dad needed to help me back to the hospital - we realised walking around wasn't a good idea. I was put into a metal tube which took a scan of my whole body. A very surreal experience, like something out of a science fiction movie, but at the time I just felt ill and wanted to go home. Happily, there was nothing wrong with my bones and I was told that my scoliosis was idiopathic.

Not long after this appointment I was given a date for my operations. The time taken, from me seeing my GP to getting this appointment, was a matter of mere months. I recall feeling shocked that I hadn't had long to consider what was happening to me and how this would affect my life at all. It was about a month before Christmas and my parents took me to the hospital at Stanmore in London. I had packed a suitcase for my stay, which I was told would be for approximately 4 weeks. I just couldn't believe I would need to stay there that long. I can't remember what I told my friends or my school, but they knew about it. The absence of easy communication like a mobile telephone meant I felt very isolated from my normal life. I recall sitting on the bed and another new girl arrived in the bed next to me. On the other side of my bed was a young girl with no hair and a bandage on her arm. I had never seen anyone like that before, not even on tv. She had cancer and had just had an

4

operation on her arm. The room itself was very long with beds on each side. There was a curtain at the middle point of the room separating it into two halves for girls and boys, but there were more girls than boys. One girl in a wheelchair came over; she had metal pins sticking out of her leg which were attached to a bar. She said her leg was being lengthened. She was very chirpy though and there was an air of hope and light-heartedness in the room, which I had yet to experience in a hospital setting.

The nurses were very kind and supported me in those first few days, especially when my parents left me there. That felt weird. I had never been separated from them before. I remember the day of my first operation like it was yesterday. It had been explained that I would have anterior surgery to fuse the lower curve of my spine which was an angle of 63 degrees. This involved going in through my side, removing several ribs and deflating my lung to access my spine. I was to have 5 screws inserted with a short rod to join them together. My parents were with me and I had the pre-med injection. I recall laughing - a lot! They said that might happen. The operating rooms were in a separate building and the porters came to get me and pushed me outside, along the path towards the theatre. That felt so strange going outside where it was cold, whilst being in a bed. I could never understand why I couldn't have just walked to the theatre and had the injection there. I remember the nurse telling me that I would feel another injection and would then just drift off and wake up later.

When I woke, it was dark in the room I was in and I just remember being told I needed to pee before they would let me move to the next intensive care section. I was told I had a catheter so I didn't need to tell them when I needed to pee as they would know. I had no idea what a catheter was at that time. I vaguely remember my mum and dad saying hello to me, but not much more. The pain was excruciating and I had an oxygen mask on which I didn't like at all and kept trying to remove as I didn't like the smell of it. I remember struggling to breathe and feeling pain, which I complained about to the nurses.

It turned out that I had a pneumothorax where the lung had been re-inflated and air had become trapped between the lung and the chest wall. I remember having a chest x-ray in my bed in the ICU and then being told I would need to have the air removed by needle and tube inserted into my chest. I remember my poor mother having to sit next to me whilst I had the procedure right there in the ICU and squeezing her hand throughout whilst fixating my stare on her face as I couldn't bear to look down at the procedure. I was so scared and frightened of the whole experience. It felt extremely sore and uncomfortable, on top of the pain I was already experiencing in my back. I also recall the sense of relief when it was over and I could breathe properly again. We had been warned of the dangers of these operations, but never thought that anything bad would happen to me.

My mum was able to stay in the hospital for a few days post-op until I was able to return to the main ward. I remember being wheeled back through the outside path in my bed and it not being so funny this time. Every bump and dip in the path caused me pain as the bed jolted along. For a couple of weeks, I was given physiotherapy and attempted to do some school work, but it was difficult because in those days we were not allowed out of bed at all and were only allowed to sit up with assistance. I quickly became constipated and had to be given several enemas to relieve me, but they weren't very successful and this became almost as painful as the pain in my back. I struck up a friendship with the girl in the bed next to me who was having a similar operation. Her parents came in daily as they weren't far away and they were friendly and nice to talk to, which was especially nice as my parents weren't able to come as regularly as they were 40 miles away and needed to work.

I remember my friends coming to see me once. They wheeled my bed outside as the sun was shining and a helicopter had arrived to bring a patient, so we were able to watch it together. They brought lots of 'get well' cards from other friends and the school. These all got strung around the top of the bed, as appeared to be the tradition in the ward. My mum brought me a ghetto-blaster and a cassette called Now That's What I Call Music, one of the first ones to be released, I think. I loved music and this brightened my spirits. I remember the cassette had The Only Way is Up by Yazoo on it. I listened to that a lot. Seems very apt now, thinking back.

I remember the day of my second operation less vividly. The process was repeated from last time, but this operation was a posterior correction of my 65 degree upper curve using a Harrington rod. This time when I came out of the operation it turned out the surgeon had unwittingly trapped a nerve at the top of my shoulder which affected the outer side of my arm and movement in my right hand. This resulted in lots of student doctors coming to look at this affliction and a special brace was constructed to support it. I was given additional physiotherapy but the damage to the nerve has never fully recovered from the muscle wastage that occurred. Even now when my hand gets cold, it clams up and I can't move it.

Not long after this operation I remember another girl in the ward being temporarily paralysed when her rod came through her back post-op. That was a very scary day, but thankfully she recovered over time, but needed a stick to assist her walking and a high-necked full body brace. I can remember her face as clear as day, she was a very brave girl and so nice to me.

I recall having the staples removed after the operation. There were lots of them. There was also another large scar on my hip where the surgeon had taken bone to graft the rod into place. The nurse tried to clean the blood away from the scars and remove the staples kindly, but the fine hairs on my back had tangled with the staples and the whole experience was very painful indeed. I also remember having the drain removed, that was also uncomfortable and a horrible vacuum feeling as it was pulled out. Not very nice at all.

I was fitted for a body brace and remember putting it on for the first time. It was incredibly uncomfortable with a hard back and a soft girdle with braces to tighten at the front. It needed to be adjusted several times as it caused sores on my back where it rubbed my skin.

The day I was finally allowed to get out of bed and stand up felt very strange after 4 weeks in bed. I was only allowed out of bed with the brace on. I had lost weight and muscle definition making me much weaker, together with an immense head rush. Apparently, I was a good few inches taller - and I felt it! I had to sit back down straight away and remember not liking it for long. It took a while to feel confident to move around on my own and remember being taken to the toilet the first time in a wheelchair. I think that was the first time I realised the consequences of these operations.

I was lucky to be discharged in time for Christmas, many weren't so lucky. I felt sad leaving them all after so long together. I thought I would be vulnerable at home and was worried something might happen. It was scary but also exciting to be going home at last. I remember going straight to bed and my parents got me a TV for Christmas to watch in my room. I spent a lot of time there because I didn't like to wear the brace. I remember my mum having to help me have a shower, that was embarrassing and awkward. I had to sit on a bath seat whilst my mum washed me, but I remember thinking that it was nothing compared to being virtually naked in front of all those doctors.

I was home-schooled for a few months and had to wear the brace for a total of 6 months. I wasn't allowed to do any sports at school and I was very conscious of how I looked. It was not a good time. As the months went on, the summer came and the heat was unbearable in a brace. It was a huge relief when I was eventually told that I no longer needed it and that my back was repaired. I had outpatient appointments for a few years to check on my progress and I consider myself lucky to get through the whole experience fairly unscathed compared to some others.

I remember compiling a scrapbook of my time in hospital. I think my parents still have it. It documents all the names and dates and even some of the equipment I took home with me. I also have 2 pre and post op x-rays. I don't think my parents still have the brace, which is a shame as I would have liked to see how it feels on me now.

A couple of years after my operations I started to get heart palpitations. A series of tests, prodding and poking by different doctors later and I was told that I had Marfan

Syndrome and that this is what caused my scoliosis. This is despite my orthopaedic surgeon disagreeing with this diagnosis at an outpatient appointment. I was put on beta-blockers to ease the palpitations and remained on them until 2 years ago when I was offered genetic testing to establish whether the diagnosis was correct. It turned out that my surgeon was correct as the test proved the diagnosis to be inaccurate. I managed to wean myself off of the beta-blockers that I had been taking for the past 30 years and have felt no ill-effects from it. I do still occasionally get palpitations but they are bearable and not causing me any harm.

Most importantly, my surgery has not caused me any problems over the years. I had a child without any complication, but I do believe that childbirth and the changes which occur to your body as a result of carrying a baby, affected my already misaligned hips and the pain I now experience in my right hip. I have had various x-rays and MRIs to try and establish the root cause of the pain, but it remains unexplained. I have been told to take regular painkillers to ease the pain, but choose not to do this. I prefer to avoid movements and exercise which I know exacerbates the pain. I will only take pain relief when the pain becomes unbearable, which it can be at times. The pain can be made worse by sleeping in a different bed or sitting on poor seating for a prolonged period - sometimes these things just cannot be avoided. A few years ago, an x-ray revealed that my Harrington Rod has broken in two, which may have occurred following a minor car accident some years ago. Not that this matters as the rod is fully fused in bone.

These days I still have the same gripes I've always had about my scoliosis - the scars, which I usually say are shark bites (sounds more exciting) but mostly what clothes to buy. This was really difficult as a teenager but luckily when I started to go out more it was the 90's and indie music came along - the fashion to wear oversize tops suited me perfectly! I have always looked for clothes that cover my back or which don't make my uneven shoulder blades look obvious. Over the years I've worked out what I can and cannot wear - for example, I can't wear a suit shirt, they just don't sit right. I also can't wear short jackets, again, they ride up on one side. The main problem has always been bras. The adjustable bit always digs in on one side. I now wear more sport-type bras but even these have their issues. As I'm tall, the straps aren't long enough so they dig into my shoulders. However, in my mind, it's a small price to pay when the scoliosis itself had got to the point that if I hadn't have had surgery it would have eventually put me in a wheelchair. When I consider the waiting times that young people have to endure these days, it fills me with horror to think that this could have happened to me in a different era.

I now live in hope that my back never needs to be operated on again. Having said that, I would always recommend the operation to anyone needing it. The advances made since I had my operation are huge. Recently, my daughter passed the age that I was when all this happened to me. I check her spine regularly and am pleased that she does not seem to be following in my footsteps, although her limbs are just as gangly!
Mercedes Macfarlane,
Bedfordshire

Paul

I never knew I had scoliosis. I grew up a happy child with no problems. I went through school and was looking forward to leaving and start training to become a chef, but in 1992 when I was 14, I started to get back aches and started to lean to my left-hand side. My mum took me to the doctors. He examined me and said there was nothing wrong with me, it was just growing pains and I needed to stand up straight and stop being lazy. My mum wasn't convinced with this outcome, but trusted him because he was our doctor. My back was still hurting and I was taking paracetamol to help with the pain. In 1994 at the age of 16 I left school and went straight into a YTS training scheme to become a chef. I started working as a trainee chef in a busy kitchen. I was really enjoying working in a kitchen as it was my dream, but I was finding it hard and my back was really hurting being on my feet all day. I just thought it was because I wasn't used to working.

So, in 1996 my mum took me to our doctors again and I was seen by a different doctor and he knew straight away I had a back problem, and thought I might have scoliosis, and it was also discovered I had NF1. He made me an appointment to see a spinal consultant at Epsom general hospital. I was seen by one of the leading spinal surgeons in the country, Dr Cheong-leen. He wanted me to have a MRI at Atkinson Morley hospital. I was really worried with what was being said, and what was happening to me. I couldn't sleep the night before the MRI, I was scared, as I'd never had one before. My mum and dad took me for the MRI, then had to wait for the results, which seemed to take for ever. In spite of sleepless nights, I carried on training to be a chef. I wanted to try and carry on as normal but found it really hard to concentrate on my work with all this worry hanging over me. Then we got a phone call telling us to come up and see Dr Cheong-leen, on the 19th April, and I had a radicular gram. It was discovered I had extensive plexiform neurofibroma to the right of the vertebral column. Then Dr Cheong-leen gave me the devastating news I needed major surgery; I had lumbar scoliosis from D1 to L4 moving 72

11

degrees. He explained the dangers of the operation, I had a 50/50 percent of being paralysed from the waist down, but if I didn't have the operation I would end up in a wheelchair.

My head was in a spin, I didn't know what to do and thought my life had ended before it even started. I discussed the pros and cons with my parents, and decided to have the operation. I had the operation at Epsom general hospital on 28th May 1996. The operation took 8hrs; the surgeons said the operation had been a success. I had a Harrington rod screwed to my spine and had 2 ribs removed to fuse to my spine. The doctors didn't know if I would be able to walk again. I had to lie on my back for nearly 2 weeks. The doctors came round and did the pin prick test on my legs and feet and thankfully I could feel it. I had a bed that tipped up and had to do that every couple of hours a day to get used to standing upright. Once I was used to standing up straight, I had to have a plaster cast fitted around my waist, which I had to wear for 6 months. When they put it on for the first time, I had to learn to walk again using crutches, which I found really hard and it took a lot out of me, I was weak. Once I could walk by myself using crutches I would be allowed to go home. After nearly 3 weeks in hospital, I went home.

It was so nice being home and being out in the fresh air, after 6 months they removed my plaster cast and I had a removable cast fitted, which meant I could have a bath. After a year recovering, I started to look for work, but one Saturday, while out shopping with Mum, I heard a snap in my back. I've never felt pain like it, so we went home and Mum phoned my consultant and had an emergency appointment. I had x-rays, and to my horror the Harrington rod had come away from my spine, I needed another operation. Just when I thought I was getting my life back on track that happened. On 3rd June 1997, I had another operation, with the risk of paralysis again. During the operation this time they took bone from my hip and put a cage at the base of my spine with the Harrington rod. I had another year recovering but I've never let it get in my way of doing things. I couldn't go back to being a trainee chef, so I just worked in pubs and worked at Butlin's, and Pontin's, then when I was 21, I went to Rhodes, Greece. I loved it so much I went back the following year and stayed for 4, only coming back for Christmas each year. I returned home when I was 25, and got a job working for a freight forwarding company, working in the warehouse and driving. I stayed there for nearly 16 years, until I was made redundant.

I've had numerous MRI and x-rays, but in 2010 an x-ray showed my Harrington rod had come away from my spine, this is what they said Harrington instrumentation of T9 to L5 with inter segmental anterior fusion from L2 to L4 with multiple metal work failure possibly pseudoarthrosis with a short sided residual curve of 100 degrees, but even all this going on, I was married for 6yrs and had 3 children. I do suffer from anxiety and depression because of the way I look, but I am seeking help with it. However, I've just found out I might have Cauda equina. I'm not sure if this is related to scoliosis, so it could mean I might need another operation. It's been hard all these years, but now there is more help for people who suffer with scoliosis.

Paul Redman.

My Scoliosis Journey – Helen Gardner

The beginning:

My journey began in 1995 when I was 14. I was the youngest of three sisters, average at school but loved gymnastics, representing my school on many occasions.

I was on a shopping trip for the family summer holiday when my sister noticed my right shoulder blade was sticking out when I was trying on swimming costumes. Being a teenager, I shrugged it off but when we got home my mum took me to see a family friend down the road who happened to be a nurse. She asked me to do what I now know as the forward-bend test, immediately told us I had Scoliosis and advised that we should go to the doctors.

I had no idea what she was talking about and the time between this and the first visit to the consultant is a bit of a blur.

I remember waiting in the waiting room and going for x-rays. What I remember most is the overwhelming feeling of shock, confusion and bewilderment at what I was seeing on the x-rays. How on earth does that happen? How can that be there in me and I haven't known?

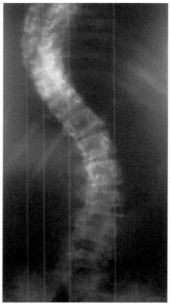

The consultant explained that I had a severe S curve, both curves being around 50degrees. Anything over 45 would usually indicate surgery as the only effective treatment. I had no pain at all so it had really snuck up on me. I'm not sure I took much in at that appointment but I knew my life was no longer quite the same.

Next steps:

After my diagnosis of adolescent idiopathic scoliosis, I think I and my family were in shock. I'm sure (although they never said it to me) my parents wondered why they hadn't noticed. In truth it can creep up quietly and rapidly, and typically with this type the patient is in their teens, not likely to be parading around hardly clothed in front of their parents! I had no pain and I think due to my gymnastics the curve was well balanced so my body hid it well, until you knew it was there and then we adopted a heightened sense of awareness. My mum was conscious about what I would wear in case people picked up on it and teased me.

So, I was on a whole new journey. Never mind becoming a teenager and experiencing all the usual anxieties and fun, I had something else entirely to think about. I was fitted for a Boston brace which I was expected to wear for 23 hours a day. I have a vague memory of the casting process. I was sort of suspended on a frame (a bit like scaffolding) and the Orthotist wrapped the warm plaster around my torso, from under my armpits to just above my hips. The weirdest thing was being asked what colour I wanted it to be. I picked blue, but I don't really think I appreciated the question! These days there are some far snazzier designs to choose from!

All the time, through all of these appointments, everything inside you is trying to fight against this new, horrible path you have been diverted onto, you don't want to be on it, but at the same time you resign yourself to having to follow it. When we collected my brace and the Orthotist fitted it for the first time, it was awful. It was so restrictive; I was stuck rigid throughout my entire torso. I felt it difficult to breathe as it had to be strapped that tight. I wondered how I was going to manage. I was so worried about what people would think at school that it became quite traumatic and was definitely a point of friction between me and my parents. As a mum now I can imagine how torn they were between wanting to help me but not wanting to see me in so much turmoil.

I only told a few very close friends at school about my diagnosis. I didn't want to be bullied, labelled a freak, laughed at. I hated wearing the brace at school, I was petrified that someone would knock into me and be nasty. I suppose I was struggling myself to come to terms with this new me, I couldn't entertain the idea of anyone else being able to understand it. Eventually I just refused to wear it to school. My parents, I think, could see it was something they had to let go, compromise on. I wore it as soon as I got home, overnight and anytime I wasn't at school. I think we all knew it was just a holding method anyway and it was only a matter of time that surgery became the focus.

Planning for surgery:

Having been wearing a Boston brace for nearly 16 months and with the degree hovering around 60 now, I made the decision with my parents to have surgery. My mum and dad were a huge source of amazing support. I can't imagine how hard it must have been to watch their child have to contemplate risks of paralysis and other significant complications. The consultant had indicated that my choice was to have the fusion, and have it as soon as possible, or to never have it at all. At the time, surgery was far less common on older patients and it made sense that it would be better to do the surgery whilst I was young as I was likely to recover quicker and it would be easier to manipulate my spine given it was so flexible. He advised that without the surgery the curve would progress by around 1 degree per year. At the time this didn't sound like much but personally I wanted to give myself the best possible chance at a future without further complications and so we decided to go ahead.

I was due to take my GCSEs in the summer so the consultant was able to schedule the surgery for just after my exams. It also allowed me to take a little break in between to celebrate (and celebrate my 16th birthday!) The wheels were set in motion and preparation was made. In fact, it might have been a benefit to have my exams looming so close, it probably helped take my mind off the upcoming surgery. I was all too aware though that the elation and relief and finishing exams would be short-lived for me, and whilst my friends would be embarking on a summer of fun and relaxation, I was facing something altogether much more frightening than the exam hall (although exams have always petrified me!).

This is it!

The night before the operation I was feeling a mixture of apprehension, nerves and fear. A room had been prepared for my mum so she could stay at the hospital, but I remember asking her to stay with me until I fell asleep. I woke up suddenly, very early, in a state of quiet panic, frightened about what was about to happen. I drifted back off and then when I awoke again, I was strangely calm, perhaps numb. It's amazing what runs through your mind at times like these. At one point I got out of my bed and did a 'bridge' as I knew this would be the last time I would ever be able to do one.

I took the pre-med and waited to be taken to theatre. The last thing I can remember is being wheeled down and hugging my dad just outside the anaesthetics room. The next vague memory I have is of being in ICU, its dark, and I glimpsed my mum sat in a chair at the end of the bed reading a magazine. I'm told about the moment they wanted to make sure I could move my toes and apparently, I tried to get up – thank goodness I was too dozy to remember! The operation had taken 13 hours during which they removed ribs, collapsed a lung, manually straightened my spine, attached numerous screws and applied the bone material to hold it in its new position. I was told to think of the metal as scaffolding. Once the bone has fused properly, the metal rods are no longer needed but for obvious reasons would not be removed unless absolutely necessary. It was the first time this operation had been performed in this hospital so the whole surgical team, 2 surgeons and the special spinal monitoring machine were transferred to it. The hospital manager even stayed to watch and he later told me how fascinating it had been! The next 2 weeks in hospital are blurred slightly but I can say it was a tough ride.

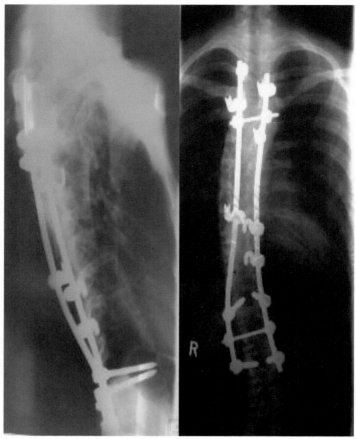

Hospital recovery:

For the first week I was not allowed out of bed. I had to lay on my back, slightly raised. The mixture of the anaesthetic coupled with the pain relief kept me very dozy but it was probably of benefit! I ached a lot, having to lay and not move yourself was limiting. Every time I coughed or breathed deeply or laughed, I was reminded of the invasive nature of the surgery. Anyone who has broken ribs before will appreciate the discomfort! I had to do breathing exercises to build the lung function back up and had physio in bed to help restore the muscles that had wasted from being immobile for so long. Slowly, I would slide down the bed so my feet were touching the end. To push myself back up would cause immense pain so I would have to call for the nurses to come and help me. The day to day activities suddenly became impossible to do on my own. The loss of dignity was inevitable, not something anyone wants to relinquish but at 16 it's certainly not something you expect to deal with. I remember a day or two after the operation the nurses washed my hair. It must have been quite disgusting but it felt so good. It's funny what little things you suddenly appreciate.

I remember it well! Seeing you in ICU on your back after the surgery made us cringe! Luckily you had morphine, so kept drifting in and out (sometimes mid conversation!) and don't remember those immediate

whole day waiting is etched in my mind. When we were able to see you in ICU your face was so swollen because you'd been on your front for so long. The 2 weeks following were filled with visits, staying overnight with you, bringing your own bedding to you, ward rounds in the garden & the purchase of a wooden reclining sun lounger for the lounge.

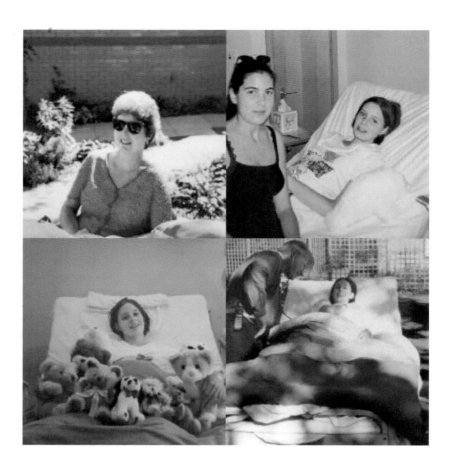

I would wake early every day and by the time I had had my breakfast I'd watched Sky News headlines several times already! It made for a very long day. My family was a light in the darkness every day. My mum stayed at the hospital for the first week, my dad would visit every day on the way home from work. When I was allowed up, he would walk down to the little kitchen with me and we'd make a hot chocolate. My sisters would visit, they even made up a little sofa bed so they could stay overnight. One of my sisters even painted my toenails to cheer me up. My Grandad would come and sit and play cards with me and we'd watch telly. My best friend would come and sit with me, we'd gossip like we would usually do but every now and then I would fall asleep mid-chat. Bless her, she would get up and have a walk around, come back and then I'd wake up and we'd carry on. My room became full of cards and cuddly toys as family and friends sent their love and support. It was incredibly humbling to see just how many people genuinely cared. One particular morning I opened a card and looked inside and the tears came instantly. All I could see was a sea of names, names of friends and classmates from my school. Many of whom I hadn't really talked about Scoliosis with, but there they were, writing their good wishes in a card just for me. I genuinely hadn't appreciated how much they might support me and even when I think of it now, nearly 24 years on, it brings a tear to my eye.

Going home:

The first time I got up I felt so heavy and breathless. It was exhausting just walking from one side of the bed to the other. Sitting up for longer periods of time was also difficult, the lung capacity still needed to improve. As it neared two weeks since the operation, I was just longing to get home. Eventually they gave me the all clear and I was finally able to get back to my comfort zone. The car journey home was one of the most painful things I can remember. Not only was it the longest I had sat upright for, so my breathing was still a bit shallow, but I felt every tiny bump in the road on our 45 minute trip.

Mum and Dad had set up a sun lounger in the living room for me so that I could recline during the day on something not too soft, but that I didn't have to spend all day lying in bed upstairs away from the hustle and bustle of the house. I had exercises to do, the one I can remember the most was how to get out of bed (roll onto your side and rise up – I still do that). I still needed a lot of help. Mum had to help me shower and wash my hair. It was like going backwards but it was so good to be home and in some sort of normality, feeling like I was over the worst and could start to move on.

When it came time to collect my GCSE results, I remember worrying a little about what people would say. I had lost weight (and I was too skinny to start with as people used to tell me) and looked very pale, but I went along with everyone else and was relieved to see I had done ok.

By September I went back to school full time. My friends were great at helping carry my bag for me and in the following Easter I managed the school American Exchange trip to New Jersey. Flights, bus trips, unfamiliar beds etc, it was quite a test! I remember my friend grabbing my suitcase off the belt at the airport for me. Whilst we were staying overnight in Washington, the hotel had a swimming pool. This was the first time I had gone swimming since the operation and I was a little nervous about how my scar would look to everyone else. I asked my friends how it was and they were so encouraging and supportive that I just went for it and haven't looked back since.

Moving on:

It's been a long time since my surgery and I'm still learning about the impact of my scoliosis. I have aches and pains from being fused for so long but am 100% certain that I would not have the quality of life I do now if I hadn't had the surgery.

When my husband and I began thinking about starting a family, I contacted my surgeon to ask if there was anything I should be taking into consideration or anything I should be aware of so that I was fully prepared. He advised that there was absolutely no reason why I should not be able to experience a perfectly normal pregnancy and birth.

We welcomed Max into the world (bang on due date!) in June 2008 and he was followed by Sam in March 2011. Both pregnancies were very straightforward. I experienced no significant back pain or discomfort. I carried both comfortably and continued to be very mobile throughout. I was looked after via 'shared care' which meant I had the usual appointments with the community midwife, but I also was overseen by a consultant. This was as much due to my fusion as it was due to my previous 2 miscarriages prior to Max's arrival.

During both pregnancies, an appointment was scheduled with an anaesthetist due to my surgical history. This was a very useful discussion. She advised, both times (I was obviously a little more clued up the second time!) that they would not be able to administer an epidural for two reasons: 1) the fusion meant that I would not be able to bend and separate the vertebrae for them to site the needle, 2) the scar tissue would make it difficult for them to locate the right place to administer the drug. In the event of needing a caesarean, I would have to have a general anaesthetic. She did mention that there would be the possibility of giving a slightly stronger painkiller than normal to bridge the gap if needed.

Armed with this knowledge I was perfectly happy that I knew the hospital would be fully up to date and that I knew what I could and couldn't have. I did still make sure I wrote in capital letters all over my notes 'CAN'T HAVE AN EPIDURAL'!!!!

Both of my boys laboured well without any complications, and I had both boys naturally without any pain relief. With Max, I did experience some continuous lower back pain for which they recommended the pool – it was a game-changer and definitely something I would recommend. The midwife was attentive, checking with me frequently how the pain was. Sam arrived too quickly for them to even finish filling the bath!

I had, and continue to have, incredible love and support from my family and friends (some of whom have been with me right through) and am positive that my experience with scoliosis has enabled me to deal with other significant challenges and upset that I have faced in the form of miscarriages and breast cancer, and a Law degree (does that count?!). It makes you determined and strong. Don't get me wrong, I still have plenty of frustration and sadness at times I still reconcile it all in my head.

I found the Scoliosis Association UK after all of my treatment but once I found them, I was keen to get involved. After I had been a member for a few years I took the opportunity to become a Regional Representative, motivated by my desire to raise awareness and support others. I strongly believe that in sharing my story I can help show others they are not alone and that there is light at the end of the tunnel. As someone once said to me 'personal experience is worth so much in understanding another's fears.'

Hazel

I was first diagnosed when I was a baby and in hospital with asthma and an observant nurse noticed my spine was curved. I was referred and saw a consultant. At that time, they decided the best approach was to 'watch and wait' - I never had to wear a back brace. As I got older, the curve got worse and by the time I was 7 years old, surgery was recommended, as my lungs were being squashed so it could become life threatening. The standard treatment at that time was fusing the spine so that it couldn't grow any more however they felt I was very young for this so they tried an experimental surgery where 2 metal rods were put in either side of my spine and they were supposed to move and 'grow' with me, keeping the spine straight. I don't remember too much about that hospital stay except that one of my dad's friends bought me these novelty pink panther slippers which attracted a lot of attention as I had these massive pink feet out while lying on the hospital bed! At that time, I missed several weeks of school so they decided to put me down a year with the 5 and 6 year olds - I remember being bored as classes consisted of being read to by the teacher and playing with toys - I didn't even last a week before they moved me back up to my normal class - I think the expression on my face while sat on the carpet for story time said it all!

Anyway, the pioneering surgery worked well for a while but then my spine started to rotate causing a lot of pain and my shoulder blade to become prominent. It was around this time that my classmates at school began to notice that I looked different and I became self-conscious - I remember one particular horrible boy decided to punch me in the back as soon as he found out about the surgery I'd had - of course I cried (more from the shock and disbelief that someone could be so nasty rather than it actually hurting) and I told a teacher who refused to believe a nine year old boy could be capable of something so mean and said he can't have realised (he did as he told me before hitting me!).

By the time I was 12 and in my first year of secondary school, I was back in hospital needing two operations a couple of weeks apart - one to remove the metal rods and a second to put in a new rod and fuse my spine so there would be no more movement. Having two operations was definitely worse than one - especially as I was allowed home in between - I really did not want to go back. I got through this although I remember being in a lot of pain. Luckily, my mum was allowed to stay on the hospital site and was with me pretty much all the time, reading from a Hi De Hi book to me and getting me through physio where I had to learn to walk again.

My older sister and younger brother were staying with relatives while my dad was working. Now I'm a mum myself, I realise how hard this must have been on my family. I missed about 6 weeks of school in total but teachers sent work home for me so I didn't get behind at all, which was good. As I had been out of school for a while at a time where we were becoming teenagers and friendship groups were changing, I ended up losing the loyalty of my friends and I was bullied at school.

The next few years were not a great time for me - the bullying was mainly verbal (which does hurt despite the sticks and stones saying) and I was pushed around a couple of times. I remember one time, this girl had decided to have a go at me for some reason and this boy shouted 'hit her in the back - that will hurt her' - I just turned round and said 'yeah do that and see how much trouble you will be in' (I must have been having a brave day!) well it worked and she didn't hit me. The threats and physical bullying came to an abrupt stop when my big sister came to the school gates one day and threatened to beat up the two ringleader girls - just seeing how terrified they looked made me feel so much better although I should say this is not a recommended course of action but at the time there was just not the awareness in schools about bullying and the teachers did absolutely nothing to help. The snide comments continued but I managed to get through school and concentrated on working hard and getting good exam results. The bullying did have an effect on my self confidence and still does to be honest - I struggle when meeting new people, but thankfully I had a couple of good friends who I met at that time and they have

30

remained friends after 30 years so something good came out of my school days.

Thankfully, I have not needed any more surgery since then. I have had two children and when I was pregnant with my eldest daughter, there wasn't much information like there is now about pregnancy and scoliosis - other than horror stories that I found when searching online! The doctors didn't really know what to expect either - the consultant I was referred to just said that I was more likely to suffer side effects if I were to have an epidural and asked for a copy of how it had all gone from my files after the birth - so not very helpful! As it was, it all went very well and I gave birth naturally to both my children so never needed the epidural in the end. My midwife was absolutely amazing and having read my notes commented how brave I was and that she wasn't surprised that I had a high pain threshold given all I had been through. I try and reassure others with scoliosis who are thinking about having children and there are a lot more positive stories to be found online now.

I know I am very lucky that I don't suffer with back pain - unless I have overdone it - the main issues I have now are that I often struggle to find clothes that I feel happy in, as do most people with this condition. I tried to look for clothing advice online and couldn't find very much other than 'carry a large bag to cover your back' - yes really! In the end, I formed a Facebook group for ladies with scoliosis who struggle to find clothes to wear that we feel happy in and we all support each other and suggest clothes and styles that may work - it's a lovely group with over 100 members from all over the world and I am so glad I set it up as although I have family and friends who are very supportive, it's so nice to speak to people who know exactly what you are going through as they are too.

Of course I often wish I didn't have scoliosis but I know I wouldn't be the person I am today if I didn't - it has certainly made me more determined and there is nothing more motivating to me than someone telling me I can't do something - from the signs on roller coasters warning me not to go on them to a well-meaning friend telling me I can't go running because of my back - I have almost completed the couch 2 5k challenge and I

31

have to admit remember her saying this has spurred me on when I find it tough!

Now I am in my 40's I have finally reached a place where I am proud of having scoliosis rather than being ashamed which I was sadly made to feel when younger. It has made me the strong person I am today. - Hazel

My Scoliosis Journey – Angela Holz

When I was young, I did not know I had scoliosis but looking back there were signs. For instance, when I was about 7 my dad bought me a skirt and was getting me to try it on and kept telling me to stand up straight. I said "I am standing up straight" and I most probably was for me. Another instance I remember was my dad telling me that I was wearing my jeans all crooked when I was about 13. My hips are one higher than the other so wearing tight things makes the difference really obvious.

But I did not know anything about my back then and embarked on a future to be a Nurse. When I started nursing I noticed that I did not have much strength to lift patients, however, my weight was only about 7st then and I was a skinny little thing so I put it down to that.

Then when I was 20, I went on holiday to Germany where my uncle lived. I was really suffering with backache and my uncle said that I needed to see his GP.

Scoliosis was much more recognised in Germany back in 1988. When I saw the GP he told me that I had to see my GP as soon as I got home, as he could see there was a problem with my back.

I made an appointment when I got home and when I saw the GP he signed me off work and sent me for an x-ray. I did not know at that time I would never work as a nurse again.

I saw the Consultant at Barnet General Hospital Herts, who informed me I was too complicated for him and I needed to be referred to the Royal National Orthopaedic Hospital in Stanmore.

So off I went to Bolsover Street (RNOH outpatients) with my mum. I went off for my x-ray and when Mr Edgar called me into the consulting room I remember my mum saying "Look at that x-ray," as it was clear that my spine was very deformed.

I remember so clearly what happened next although it was 33 years ago. Mr Edgar said that I had a curve of my cervical/Thoracic spine which was borderline for surgery, but that my lumber spine required surgery as my hips and ribs would continue to rotate and my lungs would be crushed.

There was no conversation about a choice. He said he would cut me in half under my ribs and do the surgery from the side. He would remove some ribs and hip bone and he would put 4 pins and a metal rod in my spine.

I remember my jaw just dropped as I was in total shock. He then said that I would need to be in a back brace following surgery for 6-12 months.

The whole thing was such a shock, not only did I now have to wait for surgery but I was told that I could not return to my job as a nurse. I remember the GP saying "learn to type and you won't go hungry". I was devastated.

Not only had I lost my job but also my home as I lived in NHS hospital accommodation. I wondered what would become of me. I was sent to Human Resources to find me an alternative role, and given a temporary admin job in x-ray while they recruited. After doing the job for 3 months and applying for the job myself I was told that I could not have the job due to my back, as I could not lift the x-rays. Luckily for me I found another admin job within the hospital, and they sent me to college to "learn how to type".

I ended up as a secretary in the HR department with the same person that I sat in the office with crying over my situation with my job and my home. Then on the 18th March 1991 age 23 I was called for my back surgery. The plan was that I would have T11 to L4 fused and they would then review if they would do higher up my thoracic spine 1 week later.

Although my surgery went well, I got a chest infection and had to stay in ITU for a week. I just remember being in so much pain and was turned every half an hour. I would watch the clock constantly. When I went to the ward, I was still in so much pain and when the Consultant asked me if I was to go ahead with the higher levels I said a firm no.

They did not get me up until I had been on the ward for a few days and when they did, I fainted. I remember just lying flat on my back for hours, day after day just looking up at the ceiling. I was fitted with a brace which was from under my

34

arms to going over my bottom which made it difficult to sit. Sitting however was an issue anyway as it caused so much pain. I became more mobile after getting my brace and started to wander around the hospital in my pyjamas. I got used to a routine at Stanmore and stayed for 5 weeks before being discharged. When I got home it seemed such a shock. I kept thinking this is the time I should be having breakfast etc.

I soon became desperate to go back to work for some normality. However, thinking back now I probably went back too soon. I was advised that I could go back to work after 3 months from my discharge from hospital and at that time I remember I could not sit down due to the pain. So I would just wander around the office for the few hours I was allowed to work, which also included a break where they had arranged for me to lay down in the interview room.

I thought I was doing ok but when I saw my consultant for a follow-up and they x-rayed me, I was told that my rod had broken between the first 2 pins. There was no discussion about further surgery to rectify this. I continued to wear my brace for nearly a year, it was tough in the hot weather as it was plastic and would rub and none of my clothes would fit, so I just lived in tracksuits. 1 year after my surgery my brace came off but I had muscle wastage and had to have physiotherapy before I was able go back to work full-time. This was therefore 14 months after my surgery.

Following my surgery, I have remained under the care of RNOH and have had to see the consultant, now Mr Lehovsky, at least on a yearly basis. Since my surgery, my rod has broken in 2 places and 2 of my pins are bent. The fusion did the job of stopping my spine from moving into a bigger curve than 69 degrees. However, with my metal work being unstable this has caused more issues with deterioration of my spine below the metal work. I have asked on a few occasions if the removal of the metal work could be considered and have been advised that my spine is too unstable to remove the rod and pins.

Living with my back has not been easy. I am in pain to different degrees depending on what I do. Sitting still causes issues, my legs are the same length so standing is a problem as my hips are not aligned. Walking causes pain in my hips and down my legs. Lifting pulls on my back, so also a problem. Everyday activities are not easy.

I have looked into many pain-relieving methods, medication, potions, including some from Chinese medicine, acupuncture, tens machine, heat pads, as well as having psychological support to deal with my pain.

I have been under the pain team at RNOH for the last 20 years and have been receiving steroid injections for approximately the last 13 years. However, I have been advised that continued steroids over a long period is a cancer risk (I am now rated at 1 in 300 risk) and also that it causes osteo arthritis. I already have arthritis in my spine. So now we have moved onto denervation (burning my nerves).

Denervation has been tried twice before and both times I have had a bad reaction with a flare up and pain in my legs. So this time I was told to prepare for the flare up and manage it. I have had my right side denervation and am now waiting for my left. The procedure is far from pleasant but worth it if it gives me a quality of life and reduces the need for 3 times yearly steroids and the higher risk of cancer.

Scoliosis has really changed my life from what I thought it would be. I wanted to be a nurse and Scoliosis took that away from me. I was also told that to have children would be problematic and I could end up in a wheelchair, so I did not go down that road, mainly because the person I was with at childbearing age was not prepared for me to take this risk. The relationship did not last and I am childless, and wonder if my back could have coped.

But one thing I have done is not strayed from my desire to look after people as I did when I was a nurse. I progressed in HR to Senior Management and have stayed in the healthcare sector which I love, as I now have responsibility for NHS staff which in turn provides better patient outcomes of care.

Maintaining my career has not been easy, and many times I did not want to get up in the morning due to pain. I also felt that I did not want to be open with people about my condition, assuming they would judge me. So only my close colleagues at work know about my condition. But I have also found that not telling people at work about my condition has made it easier for me to be resilient. I have been told by physios, counsellors, and psychotherapists that I should be open about my condition at work, but have decided that that is not right for me.

In my personal life I also have the opinion that your friends do not want to hear about your pain and struggle, so I keep it to myself. Without a partner and a family there is no doubt I feel a total lack of support. However, I only have to go to RNOH outpatients to see people that are worse than me and this is a wakeup call, and I realise that although I have scoliosis I am one of the lucky ones.

Jane

The school doctor first noticed my curve at the age of 5 in primary school. And for the first 6 months I spent afternoons in physiotherapy sessions, exercising to try and strengthen my back muscles to assist with rectifying my curve.

As this wasn't helping, I then began my regular visits to RNOH in Bolsover Street, London. My Consultant was Michael Edgar, and thanks to him I have been able to lead a very full and active life!!

I was a patient of Mr Edgars' back in the 70's/80's. Firstly in 1974 I was fitted with that horrible Milwaukee body brace, and some years later with the 'lighter' Boston brace. No longer a leather chin support – it was moulded plastic instead – comfy! Didn't stop me living an active life though. I played netball for my local school team, at a competitive level. By the time I was 11, I was wearing a moulded support which was a lot lighter, no neck support or visible under my clothes – rather like a girdle.

My parents didn't have the help of support groups, back in the 70's, like SAUK today. I'm sure sometimes they felt very lost and helpless – no one in my area had the same condition as me. I was a 'one off'. And support from the hospital was non-existent too. It was just that era. Families were left on 'their own' to cope.

As I have always been tall for my age, it was decided that at 13 I had my operation to correct my curve at RNOH, Stanmore (Zachery Merton Ward) and had two Harington rods inserted. They are named 'Edgar' & 'Ridge' – after my consultant of course, and my house doctor at the time (Dr Jeremy Ridge).

Does anyone remember the horrible 'traction contraption' that was fitted to your hospital bed? It was like a horse's harness attached to a weighted pulley system. Every hour, for 10 mins, you had to strap your head in and push down on the hand rail against the resistance of the weights at the end of your bed. Boy! did I cry for those first few days – the pain.

Following surgery, I was in plaster from shoulder to hips for approximately 6 months, and then back into a 'girdle' for the remaining 6 months.

I talk about having 'had' scoliosis rather than 'have' scoliosis. I have lived for 39 years with my rods, and they have never given me any grief. In fact, quite the opposite. I have obtained my Bronze, Silver & Gold Duke of Edinburgh Awards; Completed an Army assault course, partied in Ibiza, travelled around China and have two very healthy children!!

I have been in touch with both Mr Edgar and Dr Ridge (through the powers of the web) and have been able to thank them personally, all these years later, for their amazing medical skills.

Without them I may not have had all these achievements under my belt today!!
-Jane Tomlinson

Vivian

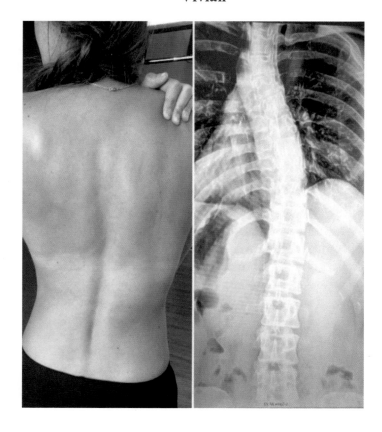

I was diagnosed with scoliosis when I was 10 years old. At the time, I had a minor curve and was told to 'wait and see' and that there was nothing I could do. I felt confused and had a gazillion questions - what does this mean? Why do I have it if no one else in my family has it? Why can't I do ANYTHING about it?

I ignored it for years. It's something you learn to hide from the world, and yourself, if you're in denial about it. You figure out how to wear your clothes in a different way or your hair long to mask it. But as I've gotten older and become more in tune with myself to understand the connection between my mind and my body, I realized that self-acceptance and confidence comes from the process.

Fast forward to my 20s - after too many twists in yoga and not understanding the correct posture for my body, my curve progressed to 31 degrees. That sparked my interest in learning more. Through my research, there were limited treatment options, so it was the belief in my ability to figure out a way to be proactive and take care of my health and my body that motivated me to keep searching and learning. *After I completed my yoga teacher training, I went on to study more about yoga specific for scoliosis, got a degree in physical therapy, and integrative health.*

Through my own personal physical therapy as well as stretches, exercises, etc. my curve went down to 24 degrees and I even grew a cm! With my experience living with scoliosis as well as my background and education in the human body, I now help those with scoliosis all over the world feel strong and confident in their bodies (inside and out).

I created SCOLIOFITNESS, a program so those with scoliosis can build self-awareness to feel empowered to live a life out of possibility and not out of fear. As an Integrative Health Practitioner, I apply my knowledge in functional and naturopathic medicine to help nourish the body from the inside out as I believe it's not just the exercises, but the nutrients, etc. to make sure our bodies are functioning at its optimal level, in addition to addressing ways to become not just physically fit, but emotionally and mentally fit.

No matter where you are in your scoliosis or health journey, I want you to know that you have control. Your diagnosis does not define you. And taking responsibility for your well-being and addressing the physical and emotional effects of a back condition can be empowering.

I started SCOLIOFITNESS help with my own personal scoliosis... and now I'm helping others. If you're interested in a free guide of 5 SIMPLE SCOLIOSIS STRETCHES to lengthen your spine and ease back pain, check out: http://bit.ly/5SimpleStretches

To all of us #scoliosiswarriors, I hope you know that YOU are capable of anything! Your diagnosis does not define you.

@daywithviv @scoliofitness   Vivian Doan, creator of SCOLIOFITNESS™

Carly

My story starts in 1981. I was born, and diagnosed with Congenital Diaphragmatic Hernia (also known as CDH). My mum didn't see me for 5 days as I was rushed to London for emergency surgery which was successful, and finally mum got her 1st cuddle.

I was monitored regularly to check all was ok as CDH babies can often suffer with problems later in life, and in March 1993 when I was 11, a routine appointment at my GP surgery highlighted some concerns that a curve had developed in my spine. I was referred to a specialist and remember going up to London not really aware of what was going on, and it was there I was diagnosed with Scoliosis. At this point it was 32 degrees, and a historic X-ray showed it had actually started to show when I was 6.

We were told the waiting list for surgery was up to 2 years, and my mum was very aware with my medical history, my growing body and the curve already present that it would no doubt get worse, and that my organs could be crushed from the curve and I'd end up in a wheelchair.

After trying to raise funds to go private, by absolute chance they discovered we had medical insurance through work, and amazingly they confirmed the operation would be paid for privately. In May 1993 I was seen in Harley Street, and by then my curve had worsened to 64 degrees. Just 3 weeks later, I was at the Princess Grace hospital in London preparing for my 2-stage spinal fusion.

Again, I remember not really taking it all in or understanding the severity of it all. My mum remembers me ordering food, watching films and playing with the electric bed thinking I was in a hotel on the first night. Mum by this point was understandably a nervous wreck.

The next day (a Wednesday) I went down for Stage 1 surgery.

This procedure was taking out one of my ribs, with the bone kept to then fuse my spine after the rod was fitted the following week. After this, I had to lay on my back for 1 week without moving at all, waiting until the following Wednesday until the Stage 2 operation.

This procedure involved inserting the titanium rod and fusing it in place with the now "smashed up" rib bone. When in recovery, I stayed in intensive care overnight, but my mum says she does not remember this as she feels she blocked the memory out for being too painful.

When I was back in my room, they took a plaster cast of my back for my new brace which I would wear 24 hours a day for 6 months.

Two days after my 2nd operation, my mum was doing a jigsaw puzzle whilst I was resting, and she recalls getting one of those strong feelings of concern as a mum, so she looked across at me and watched for a few seconds. She watched my chest for movement and couldn't see any, so she jumped up and noticed that my lips were turning blue. Straight away she hit the alarm and shouted for help, which then startled me because I opened my eyes.

A male nurse came rushing in and worked his miracle, when I then began to get colour back in my lips.

Next thing my mum knew, she was told that Mr Webb (my surgeon) rushed to the hospital (he was half way to Cornwall for a break and turned back). They discovered that surgical fluid had built up around my good lung and was compressing it, therefore restricting my breathing quite severely because my other lung could not cope if the other was not working as it should. I was taken down to surgery the following morning to have a chest drain inserted. My mum was told the procedure would only take about half an hour, and with anaesthetic recovery time I would probably be back in my room within the hour.

After 2 hours passed, mum started fretting, pacing and getting upset that I had not returned. She asked a nurse to find out information for me and was then told that I was finally in recovery. After 3 hours they brought me back and Mr Webb explained what had happened. I had aspirated under anaesthetic and sick went into my lungs, which can be life threatening. But all was well.

I do remember waking up during my Stage 2 surgery, I felt fully awake and remember it as clear as day, even now. When I told my mum, she thought I was imagining it, and it wasn't until years later when she watched a programme about the spinal fusion operation that she watched the surgeon let the anaesthetic be reduced so that the patient woke up and followed commands of 'wiggle your feet, raise your hands, speak'. She was actually gobsmacked. And speechless. For possibly the first (and last!) time in her life.

During the 3 and a bit weeks I was in hospital, I spent my 12th birthday there and remember family and friends coming up to visit and making lots of fuss. Which I obviously loved!

When we were told that I could go home, we were so happy and desperate to get back that we paid £60 for an 80 mile taxi ride to get home because we could not wait 1 more day for our free lift home. When coming out of the hospital I weighed 4 stone.

Once home, I took 2 months to recover. I wore my back brace 24 hours a day for 6 months. I remember the inside was made of sheep wool, and wow it was a hot summer in 1993 so at least 3 changes a day from soaking wet t-shirts!

I remember the first time I had a shower after getting home. When my brace had to come off for the first time since the operation, it was awful. I remember crying and shaking, just wanting the safety and security of my brace on again, it felt very weird. I can still remember the feeling now.

I went back to school 3 months after my operation and most people were kind and helpful. Then you'd get the odd one with comments like "Hunchback" and other cruel nicknames which at the age of 12 really hurt. But hey, could have been worse! After 6 months I only wore my back brace at night. During the day I was free! And it felt so good. I was never a sporty person, so it was a treat to sit out of PE for 2 years, as contact sport would prove too dangerous. No notes needed for me. I loved it!

1 year after the operation, I was able to go back to my biggest passion - dancing. Mum was nervous for me, but I was determined and back where I belonged.

I continued to dance and enjoy life, making sure I was just a regular girl like my friends. I never gave myself any limits even though I probably should have realised at times. In my early 20's, I started work as a dancer at a holiday park, and continued for 6 years, eventually becoming Entertainments manager. It was an amazing time in my life, and again nothing ever held me back. I even wore costumes which showed off my scars!

In my late 20's, I met my husband and we went on to have 2 beautiful boys. I carried them both to full term and was lucky to be able to have natural births with them both. It was a wonderful experience and the only problems I suffered during pregnancy were obvious neck and back ache.

I am now almost 40, and now my children are 9 & 5, you could say that motherhood and life in general has taken its toll on my back and I do get more pain now than I did previously, but keeping moving with walking or a warm bath usually do the trick to ease pain (and a glass of wine!). I really am holding off taking painkillers until I really have to. And I still do my weekly dance class which I love.

Someone once called me a warrior for what I went through. I guess we all are
Scoliosis warriors! - Carly Gale

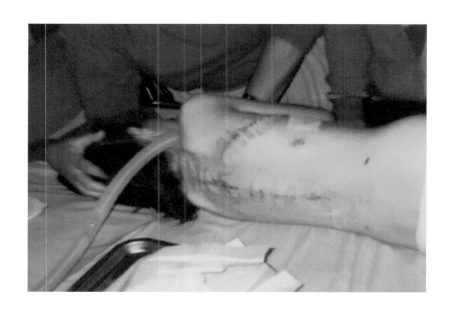

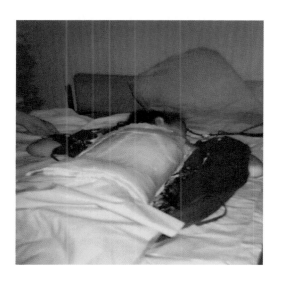

Photographs Carly Gale

Karen

I have not had rods or anything, it was before they invented them, they did a kind of experimental surgery where they were supposed to, but it was more cosmetic really.

I was born also with a double womb. I had 11 pregnancies which resulted in 4 children and I have 12 grandchildren and 2 great grandchildren. I was told I would end in a wheelchair I did for a few years, but out of it now. I also have a heart condition of AF which resulted in my having a stroke just over a year ago but have gotten over that. My mobility is not fantastic but I am fine. I do get a lot of pain but have weaned myself off the stronger painkillers I was on like morphine and Fentanyl I still take zapan for pain, but I have other ways of coping. Karen Edwards

****

Nichole

Had 3 ops. 2 at age 12, my curves were so severe I went down to theatre expecting to wake up in traction to try and help straighten the spine before they put the rod in 2 weeks later, but 1st op went well so didn't need the traction. The rod was put it 2 weeks later. Then another op at 15 as snapped rod and tried to correct hump on my back by removing sections of my rubs hoping rib cage would twist back round therefore making shoulder blade lay flatter. Whilst they had me open, they put in a new rod to replace snapped one! I have 3 children, daughter aged 23, son almost 20 and a 16 year old daughter. Started horse riding in my 30s as I couldn't do it when I was younger due to my ops. 47 now and get the odd aches and pains, but thankful I had op as may well have been in a wheelchair now. - Nichole Wilkes

****

49

Phil

I was diagnosed with adolescent idiopathic scoliosis aged 15. Luckily I'm pain free and was told that it is non-progressive. At 18 I was discharged and told I could have the corrective surgery if I wanted but the appearance has never bothered me so I never have. - Phil Micheal

****

Lauren

My story
- started to notice didn't stand up straight and had uneven shoulders in 2018
-2019 had my first appointment
Found out I had rare form of kyphosis and also found out scoliosis
Went back again in 2019 refused to do surgery and was told my curve wouldn't progress
Got discharged after second appointment
2021 got back on waiting list in February, had X-rays and my spine and got really worse
Currently waiting for my second appointment which is taking Forever. Lauren

Nicola

My scoliosis journey started nearly 30 years ago when I was 13. It was a weird and frightening time as I had been to see an epilepsy specialist the day before. I should've been a bridesmaid for my uncle on the same day but due to the severity of my curvature there was a panic as nothing fitted properly and ended up being an usher instead. Once the wedding was over my parents took me to my local hospital to be checked and after numerous x rays etc I was told it looked like I have curvature of the spine but they would have to refer me to a bigger more specialized hospital who treated this type of condition.

I waited 3 weeks to be seen during which time I was bullied at school. I was told at the appointment I would need surgery but with my age it might be better to wait till I stopped growing and it was also my decision. Fast forward a year and I started struggling with my health due to the curvature with bad chest pain/ lung infections/ pneumonia to name a few. Just before I turned 15 I was admitted to hospital and told surgery needed to happen or due to the severity of the curvature I could have permanent damage to my lung or worse. On the 18h January the decision was taken away from me. I was rushed in for surgery. The damage was very severe and my breathing was awful and had to be on constant oxygen. I spent 17 hours in surgery and spent 7 days in bud due to complications then moved to another ward where I spent 2 and a half months. I missed 2 years at high school but once I was home and strong enough, I had a private tutor who used to come daily. I spent a lot of time reading and my love of reading developed. I'm now 43 and nowhere near straight. I have learnt to adapt and live with my shape, I have to use 2 walking sticks due to balance issues and a wheelchair for distance. I have Arnold chiari malformation which is a neurological condition. - Nicola Dove

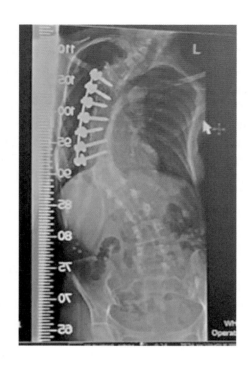

52

Shauna

I was diagnosed with Scoliosis two years ago, suffering bad pain every day. I was a health care assistant and had to quit my job because of it, which broke my heart! But doing that job, was literally leaving me crippled each day! Some days I couldn't even walk. I was also very self conscious as I had a huge rib hump, my clothes didn't fit right, I literally looked bent in the middle and I hated it! However I had my spinal fusion 7 months ago now and it has completely changed my life. I couldn't remember a time when I wasn't in agony from my back and now I get no pain! It's incredible! I'm so unbelievably grateful and feel so lucky to have this new life! I'm now back at my health care job and I've never been happier! Xx
Shauna Hobbs

Alice

At age 13 I noticed my right hip stuck out a lot more than my left. An appointment at the GP confirmed scoliosis and a referral was sent to QMC Nottingham.

First appointment at QMC I had x-rays and consultant appointments. X Rays confirmed a lumbar "C" curve as well as my right leg being slightly higher up than my left so heel raises were issued for this. The consultant advised the best action to take was to have a back brace as my curve was not severe enough for surgery and was not causing pain.

QMC appointment for back brace measuring and a discussion on how they work

Back brace fitted, very uncomfortable especially around breasts (the hard plastic pinched them especially when leaning over). Thick plastic made me feel very restricted and was the worst thing to live in 24/7. Sleeping in this was even worse, on the first night there was no sleeping for me at all.

Going to school with a brace was very worrying and stressful for me. Due to being bullied in the past I was afraid of being bullied again! Luckily most people asked questions and were curious and no one made the effort to make fun of me. Maybe it was because I needed it for a medical reason and that would be inhumane to bully someone about??

Best thing about scoliosis and a back brace for me was that I had a great excuse to not do P.E I was very happy to just stand/sit and observe especially during sports day.

Exams!! The worst part of school and having a back brace is when you sit in a hot gym already nervous about the exam and then the back brace on top of that!! Safe to say I sweat buckets and this made me finish the exam ASAP!

16 years old and I had my final yearly x rays which showed puberty had finished and my curve had not worsened. At this point I was released from wearing the back brace and only needed to return if I was concerned. Physio exercises were given to perform every day

At 18 years old I started to develop back pain so an appointment was made to see the consultant and to have x-rays.

I was my own worst enemy and had not done any of the physio exercises that were advised... fair to say I was very lazy and always made an excuse not to do them.

X Rays showed an increased curve in my lumbar but now my thoracic spine is compensating and has developed a curvature. What was a "C" is now a clear "S". Discussed re physio and monitoring or surgery. Opted to do monitoring and physio once daily.

Over the next 2 years the pain never got better despite the physio (which I wasn't doing every day but a lot more than I was before). Hips started to ache and cause problems as well as having issues with lifting heavy objects. I started to find that my bladder holding was reduced and I definitely needed the toilet more often.

When I was 21, I had another consult appointment to discuss the ongoing pain. Planned for surgery as curves had worsened slightly. Placed on a 2 yr waiting list due to C19.

Dec 20 at 21 yo i was contacted to say they could do the surgery at the end of the month. Went for many tests including blood tests, ECG checks, lung function checks and for the nurses to check my height and weight. I then had to self isolate for 13 days prior and wash my hair/body with their special wash and apply Bactroban up my nostrils.

Day of op, early morning admittance. Was greeted by a nice nurse who offered me the robes and socks to change into, including some long green socks to prevent blood clots.

By 9am, I was being wheeled down to their "prep" area and attached onto a number of lines and catheters where I swiftly fell asleep.

Woke up as high as a kite on morphine and Ketamine. I don't really remember what happened in the first 24 hrs post op. All I remember is someone telling me to wake up and keep breathing.... turns out without O2 in my nostrils I kept falling asleep and breath holding. I was kept on the O2 and close monitoring for 2 days. Once I was more aware of my surroundings, it became clear that my vision was really bad and I was struggling to see even with glasses on. After an ophthalmic appointment we discovered it was only a temporary reaction from the anaesthetic. Then 3 days later I returned home.

Being home was all I had wanted for the 5/6 days I spent in hospital. Once home, it was clear how much I was going to struggle for a little while. I was in severe pain nearly all of the time and the first night in bed was excruciating. I was on up to 10 different drugs a day for many different reasons to include pain, iron deficiency and constipation. The doctors mentioned that I had low iron levels even on the day of leaving so my medication was increased.

After 2 weeks the pain had massively reduced and the daily physio exercises were really helping. 4 weeks post op next to no pain off all pain meds apart from the odd bit of morphine when required and walking up to 1hr a day.

That is where I'm at currently. I have a 6-week appointment next week for dressing removals. - Alice Carter

My story - **Sara J**

I noticed I had a hunch on my back and uneven hips around the age of 15 but ignored it until around 18 when it started getting worse. I then went to the GP who referred me to orthopaedics who told me it was over 50% and surgery would be needed. I waited 2 years then had a 13 hr op where I was fused from t2-l4. Cosmetically the surgery worked. It took me around 8 months to get back to normal life walking and driving and a year for work. I was studying nursing working as an auxiliary in a hospital but ended up having to be re-deployed a number of times to suit my physical needs. I now work part time as a ward clerk.

I was always told pregnancy may be difficult and I would not be able to get an epidural. I struggled to conceive but finally fell pregnant. I was wheelchair bound for 30 weeks and had a water birth which went fine. I have since had confirmation that I have loose screws near t2 but pregnancy didn't do any damage to the lower back.

I have regular physio and I'm under a pain specialist and take strong pain meds. I have some mobility issues and struggle with some daily tasks but I live a relatively normal life and enjoy swimming and socialising.

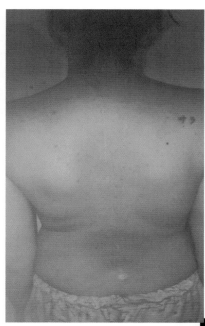

Sara Jones

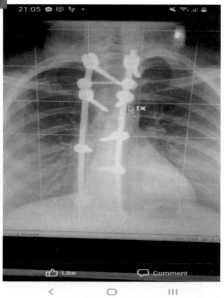

Lia

11th January 1984

I was born at St Barts hospital perfectly healthy to my mum and dad from the East End of London. I have one sister who is 10 years older than me, during my first year they discovered I had a cat allergy so my sister's cat had to go. I'm sure she resented me for them having to get rid of the cat. I was a very happy child always dancing, singing, putting on a show for my family. I loved musicals, not quite normal for a little girl in the 80s; I say I was born in the wrong era, musicals starring Doris day and gene Kelly musicals was the best but a movie called The Glass Slipper, a Cinderella musical and my favourite because it had a lot of ballet. I wanted to be a ballerina and I would do all the moves. I was very slim my mum would say 'one day you will be a ballerina.' I loved to ride my bike and play out with my friends; I was a very active child.

At ¾ years old, I developed eczema which was pretty bad from shoulders to fingertips and the back of the knees. I think I saw every dermatology doctor there was. I tried every lotion and potion going, my skin was so sore it would burn and when it was really bad it would get infected, I would scratch all night even back then I couldn't sleep, my mum would have to tape my night dresses to my wrists just so I couldn't get to the middle of my arms, I would wake up with bloody nails and night clothes where I would just scratch, somehow, I had managed to get through the tape. I was teased at school; kids would think they could catch it. I would be called cruel names like 'crocodile arms' and other weird things kids come up with, so I would hide my arms and legs from the world, when no one could see the sores/scaly skin. I was just like all the other kids – normal. I think I was about 5 when we discovered coal tar bandages. They smelt funny and was like green muddy cold bandages. After 6 months to a year, the eczema disappeared. After all the years I suffered, I was finally normal like the other kids.

At age 6 was when it all started. I may have kissed good bye to my childhood, after a cold or flu my dad took me to a doctor's appointment for a check-up. The doctor did a full examination. He asked me to bend to touch my toes and he checked my spine. I remember him trying to explain to me that my spine was a little bit to the other side, a little curve, and I heard the word 'scoliosis' for the very first time.

Unknown to me then, this word would be a word I'd use a million times. I would become this word. He said that he would be sending me to the Queen Elizabeth children's hospital to see a specialist, and a few weeks later I was seen by a specialist, and I had my first X-ray. I'm not sure on what the first measured degree was but the decision was to brace me. They took the very first of many casts that day. I still remember the feeling of the cold wet plaster of Paris being wrapped around my body then having to wait for it to dry it goes so hot it felt like it was burning, then the cutting of the cast off with a saw quite scary to a 6 year old but I got used to it. The only good thing about it was my brace man, he was nice and friendly he would call me poppet.

A few weeks later the brace was ready to be pick up. It was horrid peach flesh-like colour like hard Barbie-doll material, with some white polystyrene material on the inside that gave you blisters, not like the ones today, it was very uncomfortable, I had to wear vest tops underneath the brace and baggy clothes on top to hide the brace, it didn't go up the back , it's was mid back quite low under scapula/shoulder blades when my curve was higher up more like a corset for a child. I'm not quite sure no one said anything about it not really covering the curve, but I didn't know this until years later, so I'm all braced up, back to reality we go. 23 hours a day I had to wear the thing, I came to resent this piece of plastic, I would do as I'm told until I'd had enough, then I'd have a total meltdown, the buckles/straps were at the back so I couldn't even get it off myself if I wanted to. I would cry and beg my mum to get me out of this thing, it hurt a lot and sleep once again was bad. At times I felt I couldn't breathe and I would cry a lot. Once again, my skin was sore. I hated being restricted. I could no longer dance/sing/move around properly, I couldn't even sit in a chair like others. I was back and forth from the QE hospital having bits cut off and padding added, until the next 6 months sometimes sooner if it looked like I'd grown, a new one would be made when another X-ray and brace would be made this went on for years – 7 years in fact. I endured much teasing at school; the knock-knock jokes with kids knocking on the brace, thinking it was funny. In the end it was just a joke I started to take the micky out of myself. I had a few friends that would stick up for me then the jokes would stop. The brace restricted my movements and was heavy, so no dancing and singing, no pretending I was a ballerina anymore, no p.e lessons, no running around in the playground with my friends no skipping like I used to do with friends. I was turning into the kid that sat they with the helpers/teaching assistant in the playground. I put weight on and I was becoming a chubby kid. I was getting to the point I didn't want to go to school or leave my house. I was restricted in so many ways I became a withdrawn child.

My spine was still curving, it was obvious to me the brace did nothing for me. I started to develop a rib hump, I was diagnosed with asthma which I think was my ribs crashing my lung, I got put on meds and I piled on more weight. My doctors referred me to the Royal National Orthopaedic Hospital, Bolsover Street, and their other hospital, Stanmore. That was where I met a doctor/specialist who would become a recurring part of my life for the next 28 years.

I remember going to Bolsover Street for the first time. It was big old building, that smelled funny, old and dusty. We walked through these doors to a huge waiting room with lots and lots of chairs, a little canteen thing to get tea, with big corridors going off of the waiting room to X-ray the huge waiting area with 5 or 6 doors either side of the room. There were doors at the end of the room and above each door, old paintings on the walls of all the months of the year, very old. I believe they are still there today; when they knocked down the building, that room had to be kept with the paintings, so they built new-build apartments around that room. The hospital on Bolsover Street is now located next door. You can see through a window in a waiting area through the courtyard into that waiting room with the paintings, the big huge waiting room where I spent so many hours of my life waiting to see what the appointment outcome may be. My specialist at RNOH said they wanted to carry on bracing that they would keep monitoring but that one day when I'd grown more, they would have to do an operation, so I had another brace made at this hospital Bolsover Street. I walked in the room to have this new brace made to see a familiar face smiling back at me. It was my brace man from QE hospital, 'hello poppet'. Seeing people you know makes it all a little bit less scary.

A few years passed and I'm in secondary school. Only a few people knew about my back and I did my best to hide it. My back was getting a lot worse and I was in a lot of pain. Hospital appointments were more frequent and I missed a lot of school. I think it may have been December '97 that I was put in a full plaster jacket due to the brace not working, I had to wear this for 6 weeks, maybe more. I had to go to Stanmore to get this plaster jacket put on. Stanmore was a very old hospital, quite scary really.

I was taken into an old tiled room where there was a huge metal frame in the middle. It was like a cross in the middle with wheels ties on each corner. I was put on the cross on the middle my body was balanced on the middle pole, I then had my hands and feet tied to the wheels on each corner and I was stretched – I was literally stretched by my arms and legs, then the cast was put on – nice wet plaster cast then the hotness then the burning. The best part of the casts was having it cut off, but not this one. I didn't realise what I was letting them do. I had to stay there for what felt like forever but was probably half hour to an hour, all the time I'm balanced on this pole and my body being stretched to its limits, then once dried I was detached from the frame with just this pole up my back which they pulled out when all was dry bits was cut off and they tried to add some cotton padding, I didn't like the feeling on and really didn't want to be in this plaster jacket but I did as I was told once again, we went home and I just wished the weeks would pass. I had to go back to school after a couple of days, trying to get used to it, I would sit on a school chair and the back of the plaster cast would hit the chair and rise up hitting my chin I would have to sit all weirdly on the chair so it wouldn't hit the base and ride up. It was horrible living with that plaster jacket; impossible to sleep, and moving it was heavy. I'll never forget it was my school's Christmas concert I was sat in a chair at the front watching. These chairs were not like the plastic ones throughout the rest of the school, these were small and wooden and a weird shape. me and my cast didn't fit in this chair properly, so the chair rises moving up hitting under my chin nearly choking me nearly passing out enough was enough in my eyes, I wanted this off, I went home and kicked off with my mum shouting/crying getting myself in a state, I wanted this off. I didn't realise but I had been having panic attacks for some time, I knew how to control them with breathing techniques but my body being restricted was making them worse, I had a major panic attack I think, My body had enough that day. My mum spoke to my team at the hospital and they said I could get it cut off. We went hospital and off it come, yay !

An appointment was made for a follow up with my surgeon, they said they will just keep a eye on the curve by X-ray that was the next appointment it was decided that I would have surgery. I had to have a MRI beforehand and they found that I have a syrinx and chiari malformation of the brain. I had to see a neurosurgeon before I was allowed to have the spinal surgery. From the paperwork I have, they said it was safe; my curve was over 70 degrees. Surgery was planned for September '98 I was told go and have a lovely summer then we do surgery in September. That was it. I didn't know what I was going to have done. Scoliosis wasn't common back then and no internet to look up like today. - Lia Kinch

Lucy

Hi, following on from your post in the SAUK group I'd like to share my story.

My scoliosis story is not a serious concern as the degree of my scoliosis is very mild compared to other people.

At a young age I was diagnosed with hip dysplasia and had an operation at 2 years old to solve this and it was a successful operation and completely pain free from this and I can walk normally. Ever since, I go for annual outpatient appointments at the hospital. In November 2020 I attended one of these check up appointments and complained of back ache in the lumbar part of my spine. After being sent for an MRI scan to follow up some back ache I complained about to my surgeon who was also a spine specialist this flagged up two curvatures in my spine, one in my neck area and the other across my back.

The pain levels I experienced were not too bad but I definitely still have good days and bad days with it. I find standing up or sitting down for a long time the most painful and working at a dog kennels is quite strenuous however this has not stopped me from pursuing university to qualify as a veterinary Physiotherapist.

Going forward, my scoliosis is not severe enough to consider surgery. I was happy about this decision and although it is something that will never go away it is a part of who I am and my plan is to manage my pain levels. Whether this be learning my limits and also through Physiotherapy to retrain my muscles to support my back as much as possible.

From my experience which can be painful at times and places mental stress on myself it is all a mild condition for me and therefore I fully sympathise with anyone who has had surgery or any form of scoliosis. - Lucy Tarpey

My daughter **Shannon** was diagnosed at her 20 wk scan with spinal issues. Originally the dr said Spina Bifida only for us to be referred to Liverpool Women's for a more in depth scan. The scan at our usual hospital, Whiston, also denoted some heart concerns, which were dismissed due to Liverpool having a more in depth scanner.

Luckily for us, we had a fantastic Paediatrician who organised scans etc on her birth. She is confirmed with VaCteRl, in that she has the vertebral anomalies, dextra cardia (heart on the right hand side with 3 holes) and x1 kidney. She was also breech and her left hip socket hadn't fully formed. In addition, she had X2 skin tags by her ear, which highlights her kidney issue and she has a sacral dimple too.

One of the tests was an MRI to determine that her spinal cord was intact.

At the age of 3 months, we were told her spine was practically straight, fast forward to 9 months old and was told they don't like to operate on children under two.

At 14 months old she had her 1st operation, which was to remove the growing cartilage from a hemi-vertebrae and fuse several together. These were to grow with her and act as a hinge to straighten her out.

Now that sounded like a good idea but less than 12 months after her operation her spine collapsed around the fusion forming a teapot handle and giving her a rib hump. She went from 73 degrees to 96 in less than 12 months.

The decision was made to insert growing rods. At 3 years old she had them fitted and in one operation lost her rib hump, which had protruded 2.5 inches at its worst point.

Sadly, she got an infection and had an open wound for 2 weeks. A one week stay turned into 5 wks and for two days I was changing bloody pyjamas until her Vac machine arrived. Luckily her rods weren't removed.

6 months later her left rod moved on its own and reminded me of a pencil with an eraser on the top sticking out near her shoulder blade. The doctors decided to rectify this on her routine extension.

She had routine extensions every 6 months with the odd stitch abscess until she was 9 years old as a doctor decided her bones were resistant.

She only grew slowly in all of us as her curve was in the Thoracic region and due to the position of her heart they could only lengthen her by millimetres. Quite depressing really as she now had a scar to the anterior and lots to the posterior all over 15 inches in length for mms.

At the age of 10 they decided to fit a MAGEC rod and very nearly didn't support her spine at all but wanted to give her a chance. Her recovery was hard to watch this time as she didn't bounce back and walked extremely gingerly for weeks after. To be honest I was shocked by this. The MAGEC rod was positioned diagonally and sometimes her shoulder blade would catch it causing her to cry out in pain.

Sadly she only got 3 extensions from this as her spine fused itself to the anterior and posterior. Her spine has held true since, leaving her with a curve of 48 degrees (almost needing more surgery to which the Dr said he'd have to scratch his head to resolve).

Her torso has been left considerably shorter than it should be and distortion is obvious but strangely doesn't reflect her curvature? She's only 4ft 10 and won't grow anymore / at the age of 16 everyone's head and shoulders above her.

With all that in mind, she's very happy with her body and tells me nothing is wrong with it. As her Mum I couldn't be more delighted with her attitude.

Our journey hasn't ended here as we are currently awaiting an MRI for her neck and a referral to respiratory as she's struggling breathing but we are unsure of whether that is lockdown related but it needs investigation.

Good luck everyone and remember all journeys are unique to the individual xx - Marie Walker

Stephanie

I was diagnosed with scoliosis aged 13/14 when my mam noticed that my clothes were not sitting properly. I had an appointment at my local GP Practice in Buckie who then referred me to the local orthopaedic surgeon in Elgin. It was here that they confirmed that I had scoliosis. I was then referred to Mr McMasters and Mr Tsirikos at Royal Sick Kids in Edinburgh.

At the appointment in Edinburgh, I was told that surgical intervention was the only option as my curve was quite severe and my spine was shaped like the letter S.

Being told that if I didn't get the operation, I would end up in a wheelchair by the time I was 30 was a really scary prospect for a young teen like myself.

I was really quite upset being diagnosed with something so life changing - I had a very active life, did gymnastics, ballet dancing and majorettes and I felt that it was hugely unfair that I had developed the condition. I was also quite short in height.

My operation was in April 2005 when I was 15 years old at the Royal Sick Kids Hospital in Edinburgh. I had titanium rods and screws infused into my spine. I don't remember the few days that followed the operation but I remember waking up and feeling really nauseous. I couldn't seem to keep anything down, not even sips of water. It was then that I was diagnosed with a post op complication called SMA whereby the stomach basically closes off due to the stretching caused by the operation. Due to this, my recovery in hospital took nearly a month and I had to have a special cast made that I could take on and off. I had to be off school for 6 months before returning and I only attended for classes that I was struggling with. I ended up having to pay for my own personal tutors so that I didn't fall behind in my coursework.

Fast forward to 2008 and I was accepted to do my Nursing training, qualifying in 2011. Since then, I have worked in various environments from very acute wards to community, school nursing and private clinic work. At the start I had no problems at all, my back and its history didn't have an effect on my ability to work. At times I got niggly pains and if I was standing for too long my back would get painful along the scar.

Fast forward to 2019 - I was accepted to do my Occupational Therapy training. I decided that nursing was just too hard on my back and 12 hour shifts really didn't help it. I am halfway through my training and will hopefully requalify in 2023.

The moral of my story is that scoliosis is a life changing condition but it is a condition you can still do most things with. Living with scoliosis, I still get back pain at times, and I find that regular aromatherapy really helps with it. Scoliosis helped to shape who I am and I feel that because I have experience in both the patient and nurse roles, I know how depressing and lonely you can feel at times having to deal with the challenges that scoliosis brings. However, it is important to remember that there is an army of us, and we are all scoliosis warriors. - Stephanie Lindsay

Martin

I was born with Klippel Feil Syndrome which is a rare skeletal abnormally characterised by abnormal fusion of two or more vertebrae. Features include short webbed neck, restricted mobility of the upper spine and low hairline. I have severe Kyphoscoliosis. I also have growth hormone deficiency and Aplastic Anaemia. I saw an orthopaedic in my childhood until I was 18 when I was discharged. It was decided not to do surgery as I wasn't having any problems.

I was a very physically active person up to my early 30's and did horse riding then onto hill walking, rock climbing and canoeing. This was my way of keeping fit and mobile as well as love for outdoor pursuits.

I was quite active, that is until I had respiratory failure caused by pneumonia in 2001.

After I was ill, I lost a lot of muscle tone and was quite weak. I had to learn to walk again because of spending 6 weeks in an intensive care unit.

In 2016, I was referred to the Scoliosis team at the Norfolk and Norwich University hospital as I noticed my scoliosis was getting worse. Strange thing is though, unlike hearing stories from others who have scoliosis, I don't get much pain. As a result, there was nothing they could do due to everything else I had wrong. If they did, they'd have to break my spine in several places, be in hospital for weeks, if I survived the operation. It was agreed that the best thing was to have a mould for my wheelchair.

The priority was now to maintain the mobility I have left.

Massage therapy is the one thing that works for me, both physically and mentally as well as relaxing. I've been to the gym on the odd occasion but not really worked out. I saw a physio once but like all NHS physios you only get 6 weeks and with the best will in the world I didn't keep up the exercises. It was a motivational thing – or lack of.

September 2019, I found out about a Community Interest Company (CIC) in Norwich, Able2B. Able2B was cofounded by Rachael Hutchinson, a paediatric Orthopaedic Consultant at the Norfolk and Norwich University Hospital and Jon Thaxton, former European lightweight boxing champion. It provides sessions such as boxing and other activities for disabled people. I booked a consultation with its physiotherapist, Scott. I then started a weekly session of what is not I believe your conventional physio. This is like going to the gym but with a personal trainer who would work with you for an hour. This does cost but you have to decide what's important to your wellbeing.

In November 2019 I saw my respiratory consultant and as my spirometer test showed that it was the best since 2015, he encouraged me to continue.

Able2b also provides group sessions as well as 1-2-1. Gone online. Shadow boxing by Jon Thaxton,

During lockdown 1, sessions stopped so I wasn't able to exercise as much. Able2b had to close, at least face to face. They then managed to arrange activities online starting with boxing then gradually introducing Pilates, relaxation and general exercise classes. I occasionally took part in the boxing and the relaxation classes.

Lockdown 2, because Scott is a physiotherapist, he was able to continue to work but only on a 1-2-1 basis and following Covid 19 guidelines. This was great news as I'm not sure I could stand another 4 weeks of isolation. Going to Able2b is not just about the physical side of things it's the mental wellbeing side for me especially in lockdown.

As well as my physical well-being, there's also been my mental health. In 2014, my mental wellbeing took a dive, so I had counselling. I had a procedure in 2009 where I'd be able to use the toilet without the need of a catheter. I had a suprapubic catheter which was put in when I was in intensive care. Without going into too much detail this unique procedure worked well for a year at least. Then I developed an overactive bladder. This meant I couldn't pee.

I then had to have a catheter inserted again in the hole they made between the rectum and scrotum. This worked well for a while.

I had constant spasms (and sometimes blockages) that it started to get me down. I had to cancel my PA who I employed to support me to access the community, cancel my voluntary work and meetings. I felt I was letting people down.

Although not entirely, some of the issue I think goes down to the lower curvature of my spine.

Now, things have settled and I am taking a combination of vitamins and anti-spasmodic tablets. - Martin Symons

****

Emma

Hey, my name is Emma and this is a little insight into my experience with scoliosis. I was diagnosed when I was 17 with a double curve in the thoracic and lumber and had surgery that same year due to how quickly both of my curves deteriorated.

I had fusion surgery from T3-T12 with the hope that this would correct my lumber curve. It hasn't corrected it fully but it did improve it.

I am now in my 6th year post operation and life is ok. I still managed to go to Ecuador for a month 8 months after my surgery, climbed to Everest Base Camp in 2019 and graduated from university as a paramedic. Unfortunately, I've had to leave my frontline role due to worsening pain and a herniated disc from overuse of my back at work, but this is now resolved. I will begin work at a more sedentary job but still with the ambulance service.

The main message I have for everyone suffering with back pain and scoliosis, never give up on your dreams. If you work at it, you will get there. Have pride and accomplishment in what you have achieved, no matter how small of an achievement it is. - Emma Roberts

Jessica

I completed both college and university and gained a degree in mental health nursing.

I've worked on inpatient mental health wards for the last 3 years, long shifts, on my feet for most of my day and faced with challenging situations.

In the final months of 2020, I began to develop back pain that I'd never experienced before.

The pain started in my lumbar spine and would travel round into my stomach, it became overbearing and I struggled to do my job.

I felt as though there was something wrong, I couldn't stand for as long as I used to, I couldn't sit for as long as I used too and I just wanted to lie down all the time.

The pain would then travel into my shoulders as I was holding myself different to compensate from the pain in my lower back.

I had to restrict my duties at work and I was referred to Musculoskeletal Services for investigations.

My investigations are still ongoing but there's a firm belief from the specialists that I have unfortunately fallen into a chronic pain cycle due to the strain and tension of the fusion.

The muscle in my back regularly seizes and spasms from the irritation of the metalwork and there have been many times recently that the pain has reduced me to tears.

From telling my story I don't ever want to put people off having their surgery as in most cases it's the only option and the most appropriate option for the best quality of life, however I want people to be aware of the risks that I wasn't.

The toll of recovery on your mental health, the chronic pain that develops so many years after the fusion and the reality that you might not have the range of movement like you used too.

I feel blessed to have lived this journey, I think my scoliosis was planned into my life to show me how strong I can be and what I can achieve, although I can't help thinking it is unfair sometimes. - Jessica Rimmer

****

I've never had an operation but my c shape has gone to an s shape, had all the treatment when younger; Brace, stretched, etc, then left jobs cos of pain, been pushed from pillar to post with consultants, GP's etc, had all the knock-on problems over the years with health, had two babies, and left to just keep taking the pills…that's it in brief! Paula

****

Hi my name is Priscilla Jane Derricott and I was born with a Congenital Scoliosis which got much worse during my early childhood! It nearly ended my life when I was 10 years old.

Charlotte

I first got told I had Scoliosis when I was 12 years old. I played the violin for a school concert and with practicing so much I soon got severe back ache and decided to go to a private physio to correct the issue. The word 'Scoliosis' was mentioned, which was something my mum and I knew nothing about. Still having not much idea as to what it meant, I got referred to see a Paediatrician who monitored my spine over the 4 years with several X-Rays and MRI scans and had me attend several physio sessions to try and take control of my back ache. I found out during this time that I had an S shaped curve, with the biggest angle being 32 degrees.

At the age of 16 I was discharged with the understanding that it wouldn't get any worse with the angle having progressed to about 38 degrees. This was quite a daunting feeling, the fact that no one would be monitoring me like before. I carried on for 2 years with my back ache still not being resolved, until I gave in at 18 and tried referring myself to a specialist. After a few failed attempts I found Mr Dunsmuir, a specialist at LGI, who is so kind and understanding

He monitored me over a couple of years, examining the change in my X-Rays and scans (my curvature now being 47-48 degrees). A spinal fusion operation was now recommended to me, with it still being my choice whether I went for it or not, because he could not guarantee the curve wouldn't get much worse as I get older. I joined the waiting list which is about a year long at the age of 19/20. I got my surgery date for 19th March 2020, which was sadly cancelled due to Covid-19. I write this on 21st March 2021 and I am still waiting for a new date a whole year on from my original surgery date. Although this is so frustrating and upsetting, I feel like my extremely long journey has brought me to understand more about myself and teach me that I'm much stronger than I think! People with Scoliosis really are true warriors. - Charlotte Kneafsey

Bradley

For the last 3 years, Bradley has suffered with back, hip, knee and foot pain. During the lockdown last year, the extent of his pain became apparent to me. A friend looked at his back and noticed deviation in his back. I called the GP who ordered x rays as a matter of urgency. I took him the next day. The hospital was unable to do anything about it as the department he needed to see was at a different hospital. The GP was really good and referred him to the RVI spinal team. He noticed some unusual features in Bradley's appearance, long thin limbs, long narrow face and unusually tall for his age. At the time he was 11, he's now 12 and approximately 5ft 8.

He made a referral to the genetics department to test for Marfan syndrome. His scoliosis is syndromatic and he also has hypermobility. At this stage we are due the results from the genetics test by the end of this month. He has had his first MRI and full spinal x rays. His curve is a S curve and isn't too severe; however, he deals with significant pain every day. Bradley has given his permission to share his story this far. - Tina Evans & son, Bradley

Adele

I was 7 when they found out I had scoliosis, after 5 years of my grandmother and mother saying there was something wrong…I couldn't sit up properly, I walked with a limp & my head was always leaning to the left side. I remember a hump at the top of my back on the right side. Living with this, constantly in physio, being pulled about; doctors' examinations were so shaming. I was young but nothing was never explained to me, only whispers I would hear. When I was 10, I was put into a steel brace which they hoped would stop the spine from twisting ...this failed but still they waited for me to have the op.

I remember being in front of one consultant and being told I wouldn't make it. Charming doctor- not. My grandmother never gave up and David Anthony Jones in Morriston hospital, South Wales, said he would try his best. On the 6th Sept I was admitted to the hospital to go on control traction for 2 weeks before the op ...but after 1 week my breathing became poor & I was told that the op would take place on the 13th September, a team from Newcastle would assist. The night before, I was in the bathroom which was opposite the sister's office, and I heard them talking that they thought I wouldn't make it. I broke down, crying, and they came and took me back to bed & the registrar came to talk to me. I went to theatre scared, I was in there 13 hrs, then on a Stryker frame for 2 weeks then straight to plaster room for the old fashion plaster cast for 18mths. It took weeks before they had me to sit up, then to teach me to walk.

Since the op for the 1st 30 years, I never stopped living I have 4 children but had c sections without much problem. I never let my disability stop me living. Now, my body is in a bad way; my craft shaft has twisted 40 degrees and I have a pocket of fluid on my spine with extreme nerve damage which effects all my body, especially my left side. My foot is twisted outwards and I have a bad limp. I find it hard to walk and my body is stiff but I am breathing so that makes me lucky to be alive & grateful.

I had a Harrington rod put in place & my curve at the top was 86 degrees and 25 at the bottom. They couldn't make it straight but a lot better than what it was...I was like Quasimodo and that's what cruel children called me. I've since had 2 strokes, but nothing will stop me smiling. - Adele Leigh Collins

****

My story: **Rae**

Around 2013/14, I had chronic shoulder pain and couldn't sit up straight. This had been going on for months

I visited my nan and grandad's; their bathroom had a full length mirror. I noticed that my body wasn't in line and was pushed to one side, I told my mum and arranged a doctor's appointment

I got an appointment and was told it could be scoliosis and was sent to physiotherapy.

It was confirmed that I had scoliosis and was referred to RNOH

I had my first x-ray and it showed a thoracolumbar curve of 33 degrees. There were talks of surgery but my consultant put it off as I was 15 and had more time to grow

In 2016, I went back for a full body MRI and everything was OK, however it was discovered that I had a slightly collapsed right lung (my spine bends to the right)

Around 2019, I had my follow up appointment with an x ray, it showed my curve had increased to around 42 degrees. They measured my curve again to make sure but couldn't get an exact degree, there were more talks of surgery

Currently it's 2021 and I'm awaiting a follow up appointment to further discuss if I want surgery or not. I've decided I'm going to do the surgery as I'm struggling with the pain and want to be able to breathe properly. - Rae Frost

Our daughter **Olivia** is a British Champ level competitive gymnast. She had no issues with flexibility, no pain and so when in lockdown last summer I noticed that her back wasn't looking right, shoulder blades looked different, we went to the doctor to get her checked out. Olivia was convinced it was scoliosis. We'd only heard of this condition recently through BGT! Olivia (13 now 14) was diagnosed with scoliosis in July. We were referred to a Consultant for X-rays and MRI and was told she had a double curve (53/47). Our worlds fell apart. Our new post 45 degrees was surgery territory - no option for a brace. What we were not prepared for was the conversation of surgery now or surgery later.

We were in shock and devastated thinking that her competition gym career was over. We spoke to the gym coaches to explain. They were incredibly supportive and reassuring that this didn't mean the end. They could adapt routines with the support of her coach and physio and could support her rehabilitation. We prepared for surgery the Sept with her pre-op being on her birthday! The 4hr surgery was in Sept at The Portland Hospital in London. That was the longest 4 hrs for us as parents, constantly in turmoil; have we done the right thing, will it be successful, what will the correction be, will she be in lots of pain afterwards, will she be able to walk, will there be blood transfusions, ventilation, you name it we thought it! She's fused T2 to L2. This is to maintain some lumbar flexibility and to allow for any epidural in future life.

Surgery was successful, however, the first 24hrs in PICU was very scary. With so much morphine her breathing became laboured and she was put on oxygen. Her dad and I swapped over every hour to see her, talk to her and give ourselves some thinking time. It was very stressful not being able to both be there by her side and masked up so she couldn't see our smiles. The physio visited in the late afternoon and got her sat up, but her blood pressure dropped and she fainted, so back to laying and no more physio that day. She stayed in PICU until 3pm the following day, where we were taken to our room and on our way to recovery slowly. Day 2 was slow. Another try at sitting and standing very slowly, but she did it. No wobbles and more confidence. Pain and pressure came and went and getting comfortable was a challenge, however moving side to side in bed became a bit easier and whilst it took about 10 mins to do it, we got the routine down to a tee with moving the pillows, meds abs wires etc! Day 3 was so much progress. Sitting, standing, wires and tubes out, pyjamas on and therefore forced more movement to go to the toilet. Day 4 was more progress with the stairs and sitting upright in the chair for longer to prove we could do the 3hr journey home. Day 5 was X-rays and we are homeward bound! The correction is amazing. Her ribs are back to a normal setting and although she still has some numbness, she has coped with what her body has been through extremely well. She's such a trouper.

6 weeks in recovery and then back to school part time for 2 weeks. From the first day back, she was asking to go back full time. Nothing phases her and she's very strong willed to be 'normal'. Her recovery has been amazing. We're just through her 6 months check and all is going well. She can touch her toes now. It's taken a while and months of zoom gym conditioning but she's getting back to fitness. There are naturally things she won't be able to do (forward roll) however the future is looking bright. She's excited the consultant has signed her off to do trampolining for GCSE PE from Sept (start of yr 10) and is now able to get involved slowly in some contact sports.

I can't thank her consultant and the physio team, doctors and nurses for all they have done for Olivia. It's been a whirlwind 8 month journey so far but we are out the other side and there is no stopping her! - Amanda Morris

Everyone who has ever struggled with Scoliosis will relate to my story.It's probably not a million miles away from their own. In my experience it all gets whittled down to that one decision we all had to make – surgery or not?

My story starts with a young, happy and developing 12 year old girl, who spent most of her life upside down, handstands, cartwheels hanging out of trees or from bars found in the streets. It must have driven my parents bonkers. We had not long moved areas from a council estate in Epsom, Surrey to a bigger house in Merton Park, London, when I first started to complain about my back aching. I remember my mum reassuring me that it was probably just growing pains and at that point in my life I was very independent, as most 12 year olds are, so my parents were not present to see me in a state of undress.

Until the holiday of that year, when at a waterpark, I was amazed that I could hang from the end of the slide using my shoulder blade. Upon closer inspection my parents could see there was a difference in the growth of my spine and that of my elder sisters and once home again mum took me to see the local GP who referred me to the Royal Marsden Hospital in Carshalton.

It wasn't long before, after the x-rays, I was diagnosed with quite significant Idiopathic Scoliosis. This was 1988/89. There were hushed conversations between my parents and the doctor as they explained the prognosis and the two decisions my parents were faced with. My parents were devastated and blamed themselves for not noticing earlier but as we all know the truth is nothing could be done really.

My dad wanted second opinions and so we visited a doctor in Harley Street who simply reiterated what the original doctor had explained. Scoliosis wasn't really heard of at that time and the risks of surgery were awful, we were told that there was a 50% chance I could end up in a wheelchair, this was simply not a risk my parents were willing to take and so the decision was made – No surgery.

I have often wondered, mostly in recent years, and when reading others experiences through support groups online what my life would be like had my parents decided differently. But back then it was their decision although I am lucky enough to have parents who discussed it all with me each step of the way, unlike the doctors who aimed everything at them.

I was almost immediately put into the Milwaukee Brace 23hrs a day, provided with 60mins to wash and commence my 30min daily exercises. I was also provided with a physiotherapist who worked on me each week, Maxine was her name and I loathed her sessions. She informed me that the blisters that had formed all over my body from wearing the brace were to be healed by rubbing in surgical spirit. I remember the pain as if it were yesterday, at this point I just remembered feeling so very low and wondering how my life had taken this awful huge u-turn.

Puberty was not fun as you can imagine, I grew to resent the brace and hated the shape it had given me, I was voluptuous to put it nicely, an hour glass figure was not the norm for a 13/14 year old girl and although I attended an all-girls school the comments cut to the core, not to mention the unwanted attention from the boys/men on building sites.

I am lucky though, not only to have been blessed with a thick-ish skin but also some very loyal friends, to whom I will be eternally grateful, as they got me through some difficult times. It was not common for girls to be wearing a brace and the internet did not exist, so no support groups, help or advice, it was a hard time for us all and the feeling of being "different" was overwhelming at times.

My parents were broken-hearted but stayed up-beat and supportive, even when I was, quite frankly, awful to be around. I can't imagine, being a parent now, how they must have felt at this time but they were never anything but loving and kind and I would have truly been lost without them.

I was often called "Quozzy-mo-Jo", which was quite inventive I suppose, but it obviously did nothing for my self-esteem and I suppose looking back now, I had to toughen up quite a bit. I got into a fight on the bus coming home due to the name calling, and the girl in question actually broke her wrist punching me in the stomach, which was covered in Milwaukee brace.

There were quite a few very low moments during my brace wearing days, the embarrassment of clothes ripping, the general not sleeping and appearance, not being able to eat and drink what and when I liked as the brace pushed in so hard on my tummy. I once fell over in the snow and literally could not get up.

I think it all came to a head; my emotional wellbeing verses my physical wellbeing now coming into question. At my next appointment at the Royal Marsden, I saw a new consultant; he was a colleague of my dentist I worked for. He took one look at me and said "no more brace", he believed my spine had almost stopped growing and could see I was struggling emotionally with it all, in fact he was the first consultant to actually address me and not my parents. It was refreshing to say the least.

So that was that – no more brace. I felt elated but vulnerable all of a sudden, lots of questions about my spine growth, tackling others ignorance and how this was to affect me long term all whizzing around my head BUT the brace was gone I could actually start being me again, whoever she was. It was all a journey, but little did I know then it was not over,

I started to swim every week, took care of myself and my twisted spine, tried mostly to just forget there was ever a problem to be honest, and I did pretty well, sadly I did encounter many obstacles and exclusions to things like not being able to apply to be a Wimbledon Tennis Ball girl as I was "disabled". I was never told what degree my curves were but I have a very pronounced "S" bend, the only god send is that one curve kind of off sets the other.

I got on with my life as best I could, the pain is always there although according to the many doctors I spoke to Scoliosis is painless, I however beg to differ. The explanations regarding the shape of my spine became like a rehearsed song, always feeling sorry for those around me when my spine was obvious to others and trying to ignore the stares at the beach all became second nature but I like to think it has not held me back, too much.

I met and married my super supportive husband who literally does everything he can to stop me from lifting, carrying or putting my spine under any kind of stress. We back packed the world for a long time, and even then, he carried my bags at every opportunity, for him I will be eternally indebted. We even trekked the Himalaya and Mount Everest with him carrying all our belongings, never once has he grumbled. We went on to have two beautiful girls who are now teenagers, pregnancy was tough my spine was not happy with the extra weight but I was blessed to be able to have my second naturally. It was not an option to have an epidural but I was already prepared for that, anything spine related scares the life out of me, even now.

After the birth of my second daughter, I experienced the most intense head pains these were so bad that I considered taking my own life more than once. They would literally drop me to my knees and the pain would come on at any time and last for hours. I was given MRI scans on my brain and given muscle relaxants and anti-depressants, which I refused. It was concluded that the muscles holding my spine up were so overworked and tense all the time that nerves were being pinched causing the severe pain. Years of chiropractor care, acupuncture and physio and they still rear their ugly heads but are more in control now than ever before. My wonderful husband spends hours massaging and relaxing the muscles in my back and neck to prevent them from becoming unbearable again.

Now, I live a great life, with my scoliosis playing its part but I try very hard to not let it define who I am, I am careful and it still hurts. There are days when it's really bad and the muscles spasms in my back take my breath away in pain but I have so much to be grateful for and I try not to ever lose sight of that. What my future life will be who knows, I live each day as it comes and try not to ponder on my how my old age will be affected. - Joanna Green

Maya

When I was 9 years old, I remember walking to school and always having pain in my shoulders, it wasn't anything that worried me and I never really mentioned it to my parents as it wasn't extremely bad. Then when I was 11, I started secondary school, in PE we had to run laps of the field and I was noticing I found it hard to breathe and I would have pains in my lungs, me and my mum went to the doctors about this and they thought I could have asthma so they gave me an inhaler to try when my lungs and chest felt like this, it never really helped that much so I just dealt with it. When I was 12, my parents started to notice my back was hunched a lot of the time, they always told me to "sit up straight" and "stop slouching" obviously I couldn't correct my posture properly so they realised something was wrong. We went to the doctor after my mum did some research and suspected I had kyphosis, when we mentioned this to the GP, she didn't even know what it was and had to look it up. After looking at my spine and reading about it, she agreed, and referred me to orthopaedics at St George's in London.

My first appointment at St George's in 2016 started with X-rays, then we saw the doctor, she told me I had a 59-degree kyphosis curve and this explained the shoulder pain and lung pain I had been experiencing. I then started to have regular check-ups and X-rays at St George's to see if my spine was getting worse, which each time it had progressed by a few more degrees. When I started to get more pain every day they referred me for physio, this was in December 2016. My first physiotherapist was so nice and understanding, we would go over different exercises to try and build some core strength and stop my back from curving anymore, and she would do light tissue massage. When I was experiencing really bad pain at one point we went swimming to see if that would help. Unfortunately, this physiotherapist left and I got a new one, she was still nice but I didn't feel as comfortable around her which made physio not as great.

In 2017 things started to get worse, I was dealing with pain almost every day, I would have muscle pain and nerve pain, which made things like walking and going out with friends very difficult. I had already started to miss days off of school due to pain. In October 2017, when I was 15, I had a check-up at St George's. I had my usual x-ray and appointment with the doctor. When I went in for my appointment the doctor told me my curve was at 77 degrees, and during my last check-up, the previous doctor had measured my curve wrong. This was when I found out I needed surgery to correct my spine and I would be put as a priority. I met the spinal nurse who was very nice, she gave us leaflets and information about the surgery and her email address so we could ask her any questions. During the drive home me and my mum spoke about what I was going to do, I was in year 11 at the time so I had GCSEs approaching and this was the time most other teenagers would be thinking about their futures. After discussing the surgery with my parents, I decided to go ahead with the surgery, even though I was terrified.

Over the next few months, I ended up being in extremely bad pain, I missed a lot of school which then turned into me just doing work at home. I also had some girls from my class doing prank calls and making fun of my back. I was already very insecure and upset about everything and this made things a lot worse. Due to the pain I was in I went to a chiropractor who did light and laser therapy, it helped slightly to relieve some muscular pain but not much else. My mum was also having acupuncture so she decided it would be a good idea for me to try too, I remember I hated it and couldn't relax as I was scared of the needles moving, it didn't help at all with the pain, but when the acupuncturist looked at my back, he noticed I also had a scoliosis curve. As the time came nearer to my surgery, which was the 8th of March 2018, I was getting more nervous. I'd lost most of my friends as they were all able to go out and have fun while I was stuck at home lying on the sofa most of the time or at appointments with my mum. The week before my surgery I had some pre-op tests, which included an ECG, nerve conduct test and blood tests and some x-rays and photos, the surgeon then told me I also had scoliosis but I was all fine to go ahead with the surgery. We brought some new pyjamas and slippers to take to the hospital and anything else I would need, and I packed my suitcase a few nights before.

The night before my surgery we went out for some food and my parents had brought me a Higgy bear, which I named kyphosis Kayleigh. That night I barely slept as I was too nervous. We woke up the next morning at 6 am and I wasn't allowed to eat or drink anything. I had to have a bath and wash with a special solution the doctors gave me to make sure I was extra clean. I put my hair in French braids as I knew I wouldn't be washing for a while and it would keep my hair out of my face. When we were driving up to the hospital, I was trying not to think about it but inside I was terrified. I remember getting out of the car when we arrived and I was shaking, I felt like I was going to collapse. We went up to the paediatrics ward, which is where I would be after the surgery, I was given a gown to put on and I also wore my dressing gown as I was very cold. I then took my pre-med. It made me feel a bit more relaxed. We then walked down to the room where I would be put to sleep, I remember the doctors checking my back one last time and going through everything with me. And then they told me to lie down in the bed, it was really warm as it had a heated blanket. They put the cannulas in my hands and arms and then placed the mask on my face to start putting me to sleep. They told me to count back from 10, and that's the last thing I remember from before my surgery.

I started to wake up in the ICU, there was a nurse at the end of my bed, I remember asking her if I had had my surgery and if I had a scar, she said yes and then I asked her if my scar was really big and she said no it was very small, I think she told me this so I wouldn't get scared. When my parents came in, I was still very dosed up on drugs and was very out of it. I was really thirsty but wasn't allowed to drink lots of water in case it made me sick so I had a little sponge dunked in water I could drink from. I was in and out of sleep for the rest of the day, I found out my surgery was 8 and a half hours long and when they were doing the surgery they realised my scoliosis curve was a lot worse than they thought so they had to fuse my back further down, my fusion starts at t2 and ends at l4. I remember being really uncomfortable on my back at one point so the nurses tried to move me onto my side, when they started to move me I became very scared and started to have a really bad panic attack, my dad came in to try and calm me down, but my breathing was really shallow and my heart rate was too high and the nurse and my dad started to panic too. Some doctors came in and I started to calm down but they had to put me back on oxygen as my breathing was very shallow when I was sleeping. The rest of the night I just slept. When I woke up the next day I was in very bad pain, I think the anaesthesia had worn off and it made me more aware of how I was feeling. They tried to get me to sit up which made me very dizzy and I felt like I was going to faint, I managed to stay sitting up for a few seconds though. They moved me out of the ICU that afternoon, this was a very painful process, they had to roll me over and put a sheet under me so they could lift me up onto the new bed. The third day in hospital started off okay, I was still in and out of sleep and I managed to eat a few ice lollies, but during the night I ended up getting a really bad temperature, they tried cooling me down with a fan and cold wet paper towels but it didn't really help, this made the doctors worry that I might have an infection so they had to do an emergency x-ray, they had to slide a hard board underneath my back which was extremely painful, luckily it didn't last too long and the x-ray was done fairly quickly. I didn't have an infection and my temperature eventually started to go down. The rest of my stay in hospital was a lot like everyone else's, I started to eat a little bit more every day, and then the physios came and got me out of bed and I managed to walk a little bit, each day I managed to walk a bit more. My last day in the hospital was 8 days after my surgery, I honestly wasn't expecting to be there for that long as the surgeon had previously told me I should be going home after about 4-5 days. There was a girl in the bed next to me and we got talking, we were the same age and didn't live too far from each other, so we exchanged social media and numbers, we are still close friends now.

Waiting to be discharged from the hospital felt like ages, I really wanted to go home at this point. They gave me all my medication and explained how many times I needed to take it and when and then they let me go. The drive home was very bad, my mum tried to make it comfortable by putting the seat down and putting pillows everywhere so it would be softer but every bump in the road caused me so much pain. It took about an hour to get home and I was very relieved once we made it back. Being at home after surgery was very strange, I couldn't do anything for myself, my mum had to take me to the toilet and when I had showers I had to sit on a chair and she would have to wash my hair for me. On the third day home, we were in the bathroom after she had taken me to the toilet and I started to feel very faint. I sat down and leaned against my mum, my vision was going black and my ears were ringing. I then fainted. My mum laid me down carefully and went to call 999. I woke up on the bathroom floor.

My mum was there with me and we waited for 40 minutes for the ambulance. Once they arrived, they had to try and get me up from the floor, they had this special inflatable chair which lifted me up and they had to carry me out to the ambulance, this was very scary as I was so worried they were going to drop me, I ended up refusing to be carried and walked the rest of the way to the ambulance. They put me on a drip and drove to A & E. I had some tests at the hospital to make sure everything was okay but I just had low blood pressure. The next few weeks were very boring and painful, I was in bed most of the time, my mum would try to get me out on little walks up the road and back, which I could just about manage some days. When I started to come off of the drugs, like tramadol, my body started to have funny reactions, I developed restless leg syndrome during the night, which meant I had to move my legs all night and couldn't sleep, this then made the next day horrible, I would be in really bad pain and so tired I felt ill. I ended up not being able to do my GCSEs as my recovery took too long and I had missed too much

. A few months after my surgery I went back to physio which didn't really help with anything, but they decided to refer me to hydrotherapy to see if that would help. I had 6 sessions with hydrotherapy, it was so nice to be in the warm water, and the exercises were pretty easy but sometimes I would be in more pain after doing it. I also got referred to my local pain clinic, they spoke to me about different types of painkillers and I tried a few different ones, like gabapentin but it never really helped. In 2020 I was referred to the Bath pain clinic, this is a three week pain management course that is supposed to help you understand your pain and manage it better. I ended up having to do it online due to covid, it wasn't the most helpful thing, but I did learn a lot about chronic pain, and I got a diagnosis for chronic pain syndrome. It was also so nice to relate to other teenagers living in chronic pain. I will be 4 years post-op in 2022 and I still have chronic pain, some days are better than others but it's always there. I also now suffer from anxiety, I struggle to go out on my own and do things like go to a shop or a cafe alone. I also get bad low moods sometimes, especially when my pain is bad. Even though I still have daily struggles, I am currently at university studying music, which has always been something I've wanted to do but never thought I could do due to having limited qualifications. Anyone suffering from scoliosis or chronic pain should always try to remember how strong they are and always try to have hope. - Maya

Stephanie

I was first diagnosed with scoliosis at around 5 years old after a routine school nurse check at primary school. She noticed that one of my shoulder blades was higher than the other and I visited my GP. I was referred to the Royal Orthopaedic Hospital where I was then diagnosed. However, the curve wasn't severe then and we were told to keep an eye on it and to see how it went as I grew. I was never called back for a follow up appointment and I only really started to experience pain in year 6 at 11 years old. I went back to my GP and I had to wait to be referred back to the RO hospital. It turns out my record had been lost and there was an extremely long referral list! Whilst waiting for this appointment the pain got worse, I was unable to partake in a lot of sport and even struggled to walk home from school. My ribs were protruding due to my spine and as I moved into secondary school, I became increasingly self-conscious.

When I finally had my appointment back at the hospital, I was told that I should have had a follow up appointment and was told my curve was too bad to have a brace fitted, my only option now was surgery. I was put on a waiting list and was sent home. I was 12 years old and in shock. I was 13 when my operation finally came around and I still remember having to sign a piece of paper to say that I wanted the surgery, I wanted nothing more than to run but I know it needed doing. My surgery lasted around 10.5 hours and was under sedation for around 12. My surgery required 3 surgeons and the first task was to deflate my right lung and then break and then remove one of my ribs. I was then turned over and 2 metal rods and 26 screws were inserted into my spine. My rib was then used as bone graft to fuse the discs in my spine back together. Although the surgery went well, I did lose a lot of blood and required a transfusion. I woke up in ICU and felt like I had been hit by a train. I woke up to a catheter, a chest drain and a morphine drip. All of which took some getting used to. After a couple of days I managed a few steps and got stronger every day. I moved onto the ward after a couple of days and was finally allowed home after spending 7 days in the hospital. The recovery was tough, tougher than I ever imagined. I had about 8 weeks off school and had to be home schooled during this time. After my operation I was anaemic and would get exhausted easily. One hour of school meant a couple of hours of sleep afterwards. I returned to school gradually and went back part-time. It was a tough transition but I was glad to be back. I was a keen footballer before my surgery (despite coming off the pitch crying every time due to the pain) and I had to take a year out of playing which I was devastated about. I slowly but surely turned back into my usual self and I saw a light at the end of the 'recovery tunnel'.

Fast forward a couple of years and I was a different person. My confidence grew and I was back playing football. I knew I'd made the right decision and wondered where I would be if I had not had the surgery. I rarely experienced pain and was happy!

However, that didn't last long. The last couple of years have been hard, working full-time is a struggle and is not something I think I will able to do for long. I have found my biggest pain triggers are stress and the cold. I have to take each day as it comes and realise I will have bad days and good days. I have been in excruciating pain being unable to move and then be fine the very next day. I now ache every day without fail and have accepted that I will be in pain for life.

I didn't realise the effect my spine problems would have on my mental health. There definitely is a correlation between chronic pain and depression. I constantly compare myself to others and wonder what life would be like if I never had scoliosis. I still don't regret the surgery as I don't believe I would be able to walk today if I did not go ahead with it. However, I am in pain every day and I know that it will only get worse, not better. I have seen doctors since I have been told I have "wear and tear". It's bleak wondering what the future will be like when I am experiencing this much pain in my early twenties.

I am only 25 and am already having to think ahead about how long I will be able to work for and how I will manage to have children. I have always wanted to be a mother but I struggle to look after my nieces and nephews at the moment. I doubt myself and wonder how will I be able to look after them and wonder if I will be able to give them the best life possible. It breaks my heart to think about what they could miss out on due to my back issues.

My back has also put pressure on my relationship due to the pain I experience. Some days I am unable to walk, let alone do housework and sometimes it is left to him. He is also my emotional support and comforts me when I am in pain but how could he ever understand what it is I'm going through? I am conscious of me not being a 'good girlfriend' for him, although he reassures me continuously. We often have to change our plans due to the pain and some days I am unable to get out of bed. I want to spend my life with him but how can I put him through having to be with me when I know that I will only get worse? - Stephanie

Eleanor

My story: diagnosed 1988/89 after my sister noticed my hips weren't level, no pain at all (she also has mild scoliosis) Boston brace to wear but hated it so instead of 23 hours a day I probably wore it for maybe 2! Shoe raiser fitted but by then too self conscious about it.

After 6 months of manual work, I was off sick & offered an operation at age 21 but I refused it as risks seemed too high at the time.

Fast forward 13 years, pregnant with 3rd child. Carried two with no problems, 3rd pregnancy had pelvic displacement & sore hip, so spent the whole time stood on longer leg to take off pressure, baby born with no complications but left with a lot of pain & quick progression of scoliosis.

Finally gave in to pain & went to Dr's asking for referral to a surgeon I had been recommended to ask for. Very quick from then onwards (I did go private for first consultation then switched to nhs) put on list, 20 weeks waiting then cancellation on the day of surgery but back in within 7 weeks. Scariest thing I've ever done but also the best. - Eleanor

****

I had scoliosis when I was 13. Had surgery when I was 14. I had a C curve and a twist. It was a long recovery and I went back to school gradually. I suffer from bad circulation in my feet every now and then but I'm glad I had it done.

****

Chloe.

I was actually misdiagnosed twice before they diagnosed me with scoliosis! The first time the hospital said it was hyper mobility issues where I was tall and still growing. I went to classes for this every week for 2 years. When they realised it wasn't doing anything and I was still really uncomfortable they went back to the drawing board and then decided my tail bone was too long. They told me I needed to have surgery to have it shaved down!! (😬😬). When I had a scan ready for this surgery, they then realised it was scoliosis. At the time, my curves were tiny. I had an S curve, both measuring under 30°. They referred me to Portland Street hospital in London to monitor it. I was around 11 years old at this point. I went to my appointment and the surgeon actually really scared me when he told me about the surgery and it really put me off. As I only had minor curves, I put it off.

As I got older, I noticed things gradually progressing and 2 years ago asked my gp to refer me again. I went back to Portland Street for 2 appointments. One with the same surgeon as before. He advised that although my scoliosis had progressed, I didn't need surgery. 6 months later I had another check up there. The surgeon wasn't available that day so I saw someone else. He told me I should have the surgery and have it fast. I was so confused as literally 6 months previously I was told I didn't need it?! I decided to get a 2nd opinion and asked to change to the RNOH Stanmore to see a different surgeon. This was closer to my home so easier to get to appointments. I was transferred to Dr Leong. He made me instantly feel comfortable and he was very knowledgeable and informative. He advised that he doesn't like to operate on people 25+ due to the results not being as good as they would be on someone younger. I met with another surgeon from his team, Dr Patel, who was also really helpful.

After lots of consideration, I decided it was time to get the surgery. My curves now measuring at 43° and 54°. I agreed to the surgery in March 2021. In April I went for my pre op checks. These are valid for 3-4 months usually. I remember I

94

was at work the day I got the call with my surgery date - 29th June 2021. Over the next month I slowly started prepping myself / buying things ready for the surgery. I was on annual leave on Friday 18th June 2021 as it was my boyfriend's birthday and I'd planned a surprise day before I went into hospital. During this day, the hospital called me and said they had a cancellation and would like to bring my surgery forward.

On Monday 21st June I was admitted to hospital and had my spinal fusion on 22nd! I have never been more scared and doubted whether I was doing the right thing over and over again - that's totally normal and ok! The nurses were lovely and really looked after me. Due to covid restrictions, I could only have 2 visits a week and they could only last for 2 hours so I was alone a lot of the time I was there. When I left the hospital, the first few weeks were HARD. All my independence felt like it had gone out the window, I had to get my mum to wash my hair etc but it didn't last long. Within 6 weeks I was so much better, after 9 weeks, I started driving again. I wore a brace 23hours a day for 6 months straight. I actually got it off last week which is amazing and the surgery / recovery went really well!

— Chloe Williams

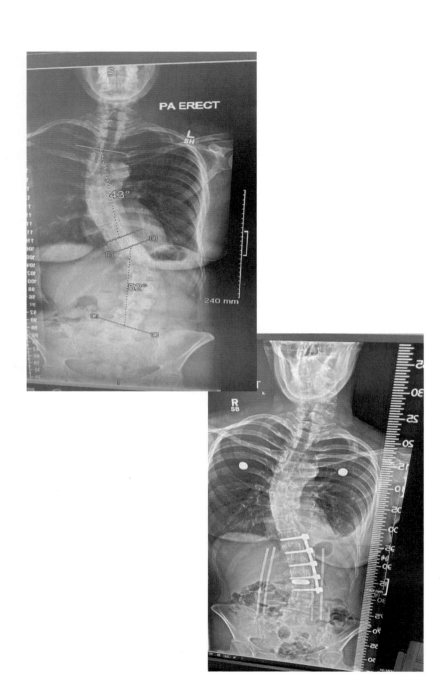

Rowan.

I was 14 when I received my scoliosis diagnosis in 2014. I'd had some pain in my lower back and shoulders when exercising but hadn't thought much of it and always put it down to growing pains. Once we began to suspect my younger sister had scoliosis, my mum looked at my back and saw one side of my rib cage stuck out more than the other. I was referred by my GP to Edinburgh Sick Kids Hospital and a few months later I had my first appointment. The whole family travelled to the hospital, which is a few hours away from where we live, for the appointment where I had x-rays taken. They found I had two curves, with the bottom one being 40 degrees and the top 30. We then had a chat with the surgeon who looked at my x-rays and felt my back, and then recommended surgery as the best treatment.

I was then given a tour of the ward which I would be in if I were to choose to have the surgery. I remember seeing a girl there who was one day post-op, and the look on her face told me it was not a pleasant experience. I was in shock at the diagnosis and felt like a zombie walking round the hospital, in denial that I would need any kind of surgery.

Once I got home and had some time to think about it, I decided I would go for the operation. I received the date for my surgery not long after that first appointment, with only 6 weeks to mentally prepare for this huge event. I started exercising more in order to build strength and be as healthy as possible before the operation. I then had a pre-op appointment where x-rays showed I would only need the bottom half of my spine fused as I was more flexible than previously thought. My surgeon was excited by this but I was unsure what it really meant and why it was a good thing, still going through the whole experience without really knowing what was happening. It wasn't that things were not explained to me but rather I couldn't wrap my brain around the fact it was all happening to me.

The day of the operation soon arrived, and I was very nervous. I didn't know what the day would entail before being taken into theatre. I had read some blogs beforehand to get an idea of the experience but not many talked about this day, focussing more on the recovery. I struggled to find people whose experience matched mine as there are so many different kinds of surgeries and curves and everyone's story is different. We waited in a room, unsure if there would be a bed for me, until they began giving me medication to prep me. The last thing I remember was sitting on the bed, feeling dizzy and anxious.

The next thing I knew I was waking up in an unfamiliar room, my parents walking in to see me and a nurse being next to me. It's a blurry memory as I was on a lot of medication, but I remember my mum's smiling face being reassuring.

The hospital stay was both a positive and negative experience. I don't remember much of the first few days as the morphine meant I slept a lot, but once I was switched to oral medications, I began to feel much more awake. The first ward I was in was a good experience, it was dedicated to kids who'd had spinal fusion like me, and the nurses were very friendly. The second ward was not quite the same, with children and crying babies all with different conditions. I remember the boy next to me had had brain surgery.

To ensure I recovered properly I had to sit up quite soon after surgery. I remember feeling as though someone had strapped me to an ironing board as my back was now straighter. It was a strange sensation that I'll never forget. Sitting was very painful and I dreaded having to do it, but I knew it was necessary to my recovery. My surgeon was very happy with the results, saying the operation was a textbook procedure, which reassured me that the recovery would be the same and that it was all worth it.

Before being allowed to go home, I had to be able to sit for a certain amount of time and be able to walk up and down stairs. I thought walking on stairs would be the worst part but it turned out to be very easy and not at all painful. I was very happy to leave the hospital, overall spending seven days there. The three hour drive home was daunting, and I was afraid of being in a lot of pain during the journey, but it wasn't bad at all.

Once home, my recovery remained uneventful and went smoothly. I wasn't allowed to bend my back at all for seven months post-op, which was difficult as it was easy to forget. I was off school for a total of 6 weeks, which flew by which I didn't expect. Going back to school was nerve wracking as I was afraid I would be hurt by someone pushing into me, but luckily that didn't happen. I would leave classes early in order to avoid the crowded and busy hallways, which I hated as I didn't want to feel different from everyone else.

Looking back now at my x-rays I am in awe of what my surgeon did and am happy with the decision I made. I'm now in little to no pain and I know this would not be the case had I not had the operation. I don't think about the actual surgery much anymore, but I do think about my back daily – how I move, how I sit, how long I stand or walk for, how everything I do could affect it, and I've had to change how I do some things, like how I get dressed. I sometimes wish I didn't have to do this, but I am proud of my scar and have no regrets about anything. - Rowan Cooper

Scoliosis, Stickler Syndrome and Me

Lynda Blackadder
03/01/2022

I was diagnosed with adolescent idiopathic scoliosis at the age of fifteen. In just twelve short weeks I went from being an outgoing and boisterous teenager to lying in a hospital bed after an eight hour operation, nervously awaiting a body cast that I would have to wear for three months. To say my world was turned upside down does not really cover it! At the time I was angry, confused and frightened. With the help of family, friends and teachers I got through the hard times and life got better…..but I can vividly remember how terrified I was during some of those difficult days.

I completed my studies, learned to scuba dive and went on to study Marine Biology. I finished my Masters of Research and now work as an Inshore Fisheries Advisor for Marine Scotland Science. My career has allowed me to travel the world, spend weeks at sea, quad bike along beautiful beaches, and visit amazing locations around Scotland.

I should also mention that I have sky dived from 12000ft, abseiled down rock faces and white water rafted, all with titanium rods in my spine! I have always been an outgoing person and I am so pleased that my surgery has not stopped me from achieving my goals.

My proudest and happiest of moments all involve my family. I got married in 2012 and now have two children. I am extremely close to my family and I really can't express enough how their love and support have helped me to tackle the challenges that I have faced.

However, it has not always been easy or pain free. I did start to have issues with my joints (I think I was around 26). I always knew I was "bendy" and a lot more flexible than most people. I found that my shoulders and hips were dislocating much more frequently and would often "pop-out" whilst I was sleeping. This would leave me in considerable pain and I would feel achy and extremely tired for the rest of the day.

My GP refereed me to an excellent rheumatologist who quickly recognized the high degree of my "hypermobility" and got me started at physiotherapy. The exercises started to make a difference and I attended a modified pilates class on a weekly basis.

At the same time, I was referred to a geneticist and orthopedic surgeon. I was already aware of Marfans syndrome but I had no idea that other connective tissue disorders were linked to scoliosis.

My long limbs, hypermobility, short sightedness, previous hole in retina, high palate and skin type could be indicative of Marfan, Stickler or Ehlers-Danlos syndrome (to name just a few!). Many of these syndromes have similar features which often overlap. My mum, sister and I were tested for Marfans, but this came back negative. Instead, the geneticist has diagnosed us with Stickler Syndrome, which mainly affects the collagen tissue in our bodies.

The orthopedic surgeon was quite amazed at the degree of flexibility in my shoulders and hips; he was able to dislocate both shoulders in all directions! The surgeon explained that surgery was not the best option in my case because the ligaments around the joint are too stretchy and if they operated to tighten these around the joint then I would lose mobility, and then the chances that the ligaments would simply stretch again are very high.

My best course of action is to keep up the physiotherapy and pilates exercises and to be aware of what my joints are doing. For example, I consciously hold my shoulders and knees in place in place whether I am standing or sitting. These issues did pose considerable problems during both of my pregnancies, as your body relaxes and prepares for birth. I had to use crutches from a very early stage and my pelvis kept separating. My pregnancies were over seen by an excellent group of clinicians and both children arrived early (induction at 37 weeks) but naturally.

I am writing this because I wish I had known about these syndromes. If I had been made aware of my hypermobility then I could have been attending physiotherapy and my joints might not be in such a bad way now. I want fellow scoliosis patients to have a look at the features of these syndromes and discuss any worries with their doctors.

I also want people to understand that a life with scoliosis means different things for different people. There will be choices that you (or your parents) will have to make and I think that you should not make these in isolation. Find out information, expand your knowledge and talk to people. Ask questions, clarify and then reframe to consider all of the possibilities for any available treatment available.

Take one day at a time but try to keep a positive mind set to achieve your goals, and surround yourself with people who want to help you. I wish you luck on your journey.

Kayleigh

I was diagnosed at 10 years old after a lot of back and forth to different doctors and my parents pleading with them that something was wrong with me. They attempted a Boston brace but by the time it was made my curve had gotten a lot worse, and it was decided surgery was my best option. I was operated on at the University of Wales Hospital when I was 12 years old, as my curve had gotten considerably worse and was putting pressure on my lungs. I had to have a fill fusion, which took 8 hours. I had titanium rods placed either side of my spine, and some ribs removed and fused into my spine. The surgery was successful and 3 months later I was back in school. However, I have lived in pain ever since and it has got worse as I've got older. I've been to see a number of doctors, who sent me for physiotherapy that did absolutely nothing for me. I found that the after care was very poor after I had the surgery, I was sent home 8 days after the surgery and received no support after that. But despite the pain, I gave birth to a beautiful daughter 3 months ago who has lightened my life. Kayleigh

Juliette

I was born in 1964 out of wedlock with a cleft lip I was brought up by my grandparents but always had my narcissistic, mental abusing Mother in the background.

It was not until I was 13/14 that the doctor noticed my scoliosis. I was sent to physio to do some exercises but never really bothered (typical teenager)

I had some deep burning pain from time to time but it paled into insignificance as I had a harder time dealing with my mental health issues and just got on with it. I even started weight training at the age of 19. Not because of my back but help my mental state after a breakdown

It became a bit of an addiction and was just about to go into competitions when my life took another turn and I stopped

Scoliosis never stopped me from working, I even had two children with no pain relief. The doctors say I have a very high pain threshold

I never really focused on it and to me, it just looked like I had a shoulder blade sticking out slightly. If I was in a crowd and someone brushed past me and caught my shoulder blade, now that would hurt

It wasn't until 6 years ago my sister and I were comparing our scoliosis experiences (she too got diagnosed at 14) that I saw what my back actually looked like. She bent over and I saw a huge hump. I bent over and my brother said mine was a lot bigger 😲😲

I was a little in shock. Yes, I had seen my X-ray but I was younger and didn't really comprehend. Is that what people see when they are behind me?

As I have got older the pain is getting stronger and two years ago I gave up/sold my three businesses

Someone said I should be able to get PIP and or disability allowance.

Wow, what a mistake that was. I was assessed for PIP by a "health professional" whose son had scoliosis strangely enough and when I got my results back I thought they mixed me up with someone else. She said I wasn't eligible and had no problems (to cut a long story very short) 😕

I went to be assessed for disability allowance and the same result. Only to say we all get backache from time to time

My husband and I were on Universal Credit thanks to Covid and even my "work coach" although sympathetic at times dismissed my condition and continues to go on about her pain when she had her hip shattered when she fell off her horse

All this made me feel like I was a liar and that's a massive trigger for me.

My mental health suffered yet again

During Covid, my husband and I were able to concentrate on a project that we dreamed of...film production. We have gone on to win award-winning films and music videos which was a great diversion and I can stop and start or have a break when I need to but unfortunately, it does not bring money into the house. It's only the likes of Mendes, Speilburg and Ritchie that earn the money 😕😝

So this is a new year and a new start and I will never give in to either my back issues or mental health issues

I will most likely restart my therapy business again, but on a small scale compared to last time

I still exercise and use weights to hopefully keep some muscle tone and hold me up so to speak

I feel for the ones that get consumed with the pain and struggle with their mobility

I class myself lucky and maybe my mental health issues were a distraction from the pain. I was too busy trying to deal with the pain in my head and heart. Juliette

Lucy

Lucy was diagnosed with a potential problem when I was 20 weeks pregnant- she was found to have agenesis of corpus callosum (bundle of nerves missing in brain) so had grossly enlarged ventricles in her brain. She was also found to have a hemivertebra at t11-t12

From her being born she was monitored regularly by the team at Leeds general infirmary under the care of Mr Rao.

Age 8 we had bloods tested for genetic issues and she was found to have trisomy 8 mosaicism which probably accounts for both abnormalities as well as a few others!

When Lucy was 9 her curve changed from 49° to 62° quite quickly and she was experiencing more back pain/ her curve was not typical s shaped so she developed a large rib hump and it was pushing inward- so 10th June 2019 age 10 she had fusion t5- l5 .

She was in hospital 6 days and was amazing- immediately grew 5cm in height post operatively.

Lucy is now 14 and whilst she hasn't returned to ballet, her operation has enabled her to be completely pain free so far. She is year 9 and whilst academic stuff can be a struggle she has been blessed with skills of empathy and care for others.

We are thankful to God for the timings of her surgery and His hand over the surgeons giving them wisdom.

These are her words....

Hi my name is Lucy Macleod, age 14, and this is my experience with scoliosis. For me, scoliosis is not a weakness but an advantage, because no one can do things I can do, like have a family that supports me every single step. Since I had spinal surgery at Leeds general infirmary correcting my spine, it gave me another path of choice to be like some people at school but I always know that I am unique and different to all the rest. My surgery could have gone lots of ways but I was in great hands with the surgeons who knew what was going to happen. After my surgery on the 10th of June 2019 my life changed faster than I expected because I could not do swimming or ballet until I was given the all clear and I missed a bit of year six after my days on recovery but still my best friends never forgot about me and wished me a lovely farewell before they could see me once again. Today I am trying my best in classes at secondary school and never accept defeat on challenges I could never think of doing.   Rachel and Lucy

Charmaine

My journey started age 47. I had a significant kyphosis curve also scoliosis & cervical kyphosis, my first surgery was February 2017 and it didn't go so well.

After a week of being in agony in hospital I was rushed down for an emergency MRI. Two bottom screws had come loose, so back in surgery to have an extension bar put in to L2 , I found recovery difficult as I also have Ethler Danlos syndrome. After a few months I noticed my kyphosis curve was returning and was told I had proximal junctional kyphosis. I was left for a while and my screws started to protrude out my back making me look like a dinosaur. I was devastated, so a 3rd surgery was scheduled in the November, where extra screws were placed in my neck. Unfortunately, this didn't work either as months later my neck collapsed and all the top screws ripped away. I've never known pain like it. I was rushed to my local hospital where they kept me in a collar until they could reach my surgeon, a hospital 200 miles from my home as I live in Yorkshire but I was treated at a spinal hospital in Stanmore London.

I was then booked in for what would now be my 4th surgery, but before he could continue, I was placed in traction for around 8 weeks. Not being able to move, looking at the ceiling, feeling like my head was literally being ripped off my neck was like being in a movie on a torture rack 😕. After traction I was taken into surgery again, where this time my neck was wired together instead of using screws, I was placed in a halo brace 6 months, this caused me extreme depression, I couldn't bath, wash my hair, I couldn't sleep as had to sleep upright, it was heavy, uncomfortable, hot and itchy; the worst time in my life. The pain is indescribable 😕.

It's been a couple of years now and my mental health has improved, but I'm in constant pain , I'm now waiting on an appointment on the 20th January as my screws have yet again started to protrude, it's seems like a never ending journey for me , but having Ethler Danlos syndrome causes major issues and having osteopenia , osteophytes , and my age doesn't help I'm now 51. Charmaine

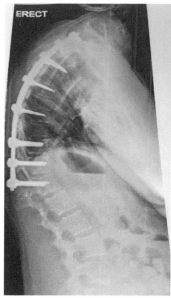

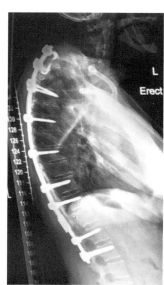

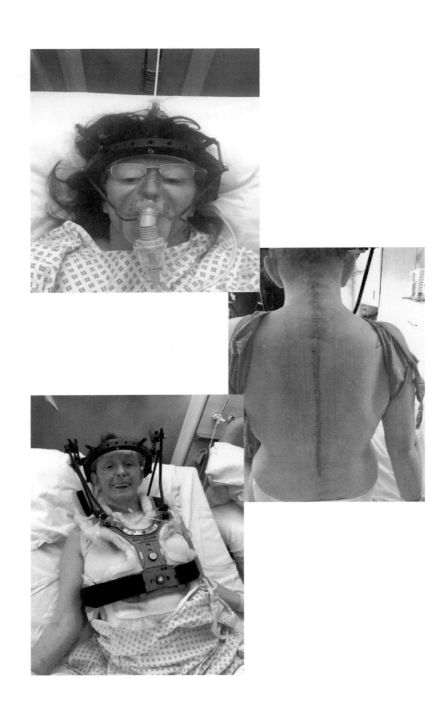

Leah

My name is Leah, I have infantile thoracic scoliosis. I was diagnosed at 10 months old. I had a plaster cast brace and neck support; however, my curve was progressing too quickly and so I two spinal surgeries at age 5. During the surgery bone was placed between the vertebra of my spine to try and prevent my curve from progressing further, unfortunately this did not work as hoped.

I have kyphosis and my spine is S shaped, with two curves, one measuring at around 108 degrees. I have been seen by a number of consultants and have had enough x-rays and MRI's to fill a library, unfortunately the risk paralysis if further surgery were tried is too high. The result of the surgery is also thought to maybe reduce the lump on my back by half an inch – I think you will agree to benefits do not outweigh the risks! My scoliosis can be painful and has reduced my body height, lung capacity and upper body strength. Having said this, I lead a "normal" life, I work full time, drive a manual car and I enjoy everyday things and have even travelled the world alone. I try to manage my pain by keeping active, going to the gym, walking and have recently start Pilates.

One of the biggest challenges can be the public, I look physically different and receive comments and looks from others on a daily basis. Therefore, I have joined a local scoliosis support group and am aiming try to promote awareness of scoliosis. I have shared my story with my works newsletter and created a video about my scoliosis that I shared on social media. As my scoliosis is very severe, I want to show people that this diagnosis shouldn't hold them back and that they can lead a great life! Every day I am very grateful that I have the ability to walk, talk, hear and see, I am grateful to be able to work and support myself in my own home. I want people to be proud and empowered by their scars from their surgery and realise that scars are a normal part of life and that having a scar or scoliosis should not stop them from being who they are and doing what

they want to do! Be you, be proud, flaunt your quirks, scars and imperfect
perfections!

My name is Emily Pritchard I am 26 years old and I was diagnosed with scoliosis a year ago.

Growing up I always felt off kilter but put it down to various excuses. Even when I was often having to lay on the floor to reduce back pain, I gave myself excuses like "I was sat at my desk for too long" or "I was standing for too long", completely contrasting excuses but I only viewed it as that day's issue and not realising how often I was having this excruciating back pain.

Like many I was doing home workouts during lockdown and furlough. In December 2020 my shoulder popped out when doing burpees, like it has done many times before. Only this time, a few days later, I noticed swelling on one side of my back. After getting a phone call appointment (8th December) with my doctor's surgery for that day, I was able to talk to the doctor who asked me to come down as soon as I could for a physical examination. I cannot explain how lucky I am to have a doctor's surgery that answers the phones and allows people to attend the surgery even during the crazy year that we had been having.

Upon arrival the doctor felt my back and then asked me to bend over at the waist, which to me at the time sounded like the weirdest position but now I know it is the easiest way to see

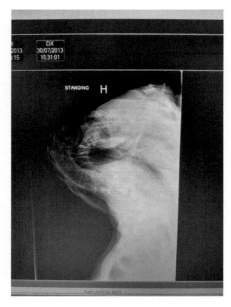

with the human eye if there is any unevenness with the spine. She saw a deformity and asked if I had ever been tested for scoliosis. I recalled that when I was around 14 someone in my church told my mum to get me tested for scoliosis and when I went to my local doctor's surgery at that time (different doctors' surgery) all the doctor did was look at me and tell me I didn't have it. They didn't feel along my spine and they didn't get me to bend over at my waist. I can only imagine how different my life would be now.

Two weeks later after my appointment, 22nd December, I had an X-ray on my spine at my local hospital. I still remember sitting in the waiting area and seeing people with casts on their body and me "looking normal", thinking I didn't belong here as I wasn't injured. Feeling exposed in the gaping hospital gowns for the x-ray, and the gentleman operating the x-ray machine, saying that he will send my doctor the results of the scan and somehow knowing there was something there.

As you can imagine the rest of my year, I researched all about scoliosis. The different types, C shaped and S shaped, the levels of severity in the degrees of curvature. Some things started to make sense in my research, the uneven waist shapes, one shoulder higher than the other and lower back pain. But even so, because I couldn't see any deformity (I was picturing the Hunchback of Notre Dame) I thought I would only have the C shaped scoliosis and only a small degree of curve.

On the 7th January I had the phone call with my doctor regarding the results of the x-ray. She confirmed I had scoliosis and that it was S shaped, a shock to myself as I know that normally comes with the easiest to view deformities. She also advised that she was referring me to the local Scoliosis hospital for physio and that I will find out more about my scoliosis.

The 18th February I had my appointment at the Royal National Orthopaedic Hospital in Bolsover Street. Due to the pandemic, I took advantage of the quiet roads and was driven up by my sister. Fortunately, we left lots of time to get there as when I arrived, I found a missed call asking me to go in earlier than planned to have a more in depth x-ray. I had the x-ray and then spoke to my consultant who did a full physical examination, checking my movement, reflexes and what pain or limitations I have had. I have a 32 degree lumbar curve and thoracic curve.

Since February I have been having physio every 3 weeks, some in person (especially at the beginning) and some virtual appointments. My therapist is amazing, not only has she given me the exercises to use but she has answered so many questions that I've had. Explained that my hypermobility along with scoliosis has caused various body parts to pop out, the shoulder primarily but my jaw and thumbs have too. Given me the tools on how to continue living life without limitations, all I must do is adjust it to how my body works.

I cannot fault the service I received by my current doctor, the consultant or physio therapist. I only wish I had been diagnosed when I was 14, as I would have been put into a back brace to reduce the curvature. For now, I will continue with my physio until I get my next x-ray in July to find out what my future will be, whether I continue with the exercises I've been given, or find out my curvature has worsened, and I will need spinal fusion.

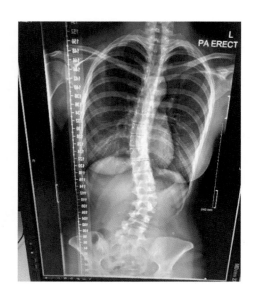

Caroline Freedman - Author, Health Writer and Personal Trainer - @scoliosishandbook

When Tia asked me to write something for her Scoliosis Stories book, I really struggled to decide if I wanted to write how scoliosis has affected me long term. As the author of The Scoliosis Handbook of Safe and Effective Exercises Pre and Post Surgery, my book has become the go-to for advice in relation to which exercises are safe and which to avoid after surgery.

When I wrote the book, I really wanted it to be upbeat and not to scare anyone. It is a positive book about recovery and determination. However, though I can speak for hours about the physical side of things, talking about my mental health struggle that comes with scoliosis is where I have kept quiet.

So where do I start.......

I have two children. I was advised not to have any more but I believe that was incorrect and I think I would have been fine with one or two more pregnancies. At 55 years old it's a bit late now! That is very personal and other people may take a different view of any risk including softening of the ligaments while pregnant etc.

116

It's really made me think about how I actually feel. I was interviewed by the Scoliosis Association UK and during our conversations I realised that when anyone asked me how I was feeling I related that to my physical health and not my mental health. I dealt with having surgery, losing my ability to work as a pattern cutter (I was a design and pattern cutting student at London College of Fashion at the time) and the life change of spinal fusion surgery by blocking it out and getting on with things. I think there is a lot to be said in using this coping strategy.....until one day years later you realise that stuff needs to be dealt with.

When I had surgery there was no emotional support offered. All the younger scoliosis patients I now see are given counselling as routine. There was no Facebook or Instagram. I find Instagram a much more positive platform as Facebook is often full of negative experiences rather than evenly balanced.

I have had three surgeries.

One at age 20, second age 22 and most recently when I was 47. The middle surgery was due to rod breakage and the latter due to my spine deciding to rotate so I looked like a shark from the back. (This is rare before anyone starts to panic it may happen to them)

So....now I have to get to the nitty gritty. Scoliosis has been a pain in the back! You don't want to moan but it's annoying. Last night I swapped places with my husband at dinner as I was having to rotate to speak to him sitting on the corner of a bar table in my favourite swanky restaurant as I was uncomfortable. Then I realised that during COVID they had 'upgraded the bar stools', unfortunately a 'downgrade' for me! The seat sloped backwards and the back was the wrong shape, I'm sure many of you can relate to this.

I'm still avoiding how scoliosis has affected me - as let's face it - a chair is not really a major issue, it's just annoying.

Hard as it is to speak about, I think that my body image has been hugely affected. What I look like from my left or right side is different, even with a good correction. I still have a curve

117

and I'm sure that if I started my surgery journey now, I would be more symmetrical. I do think eating disorders are rife with scoliosis patients. Mine is mild and controlled after I eventually sought counselling in my late 30's.

Speaking to other people with scoliosis, I realise that diet, body image and self confidence affects each of us and there does need to be more support.

Over the years I've learned to accept my unsymmetrical body. Most of us are so hyper critical when it comes to ourselves, yet as I say to many of my clients who are so self conscious - look around, what do you see? Do you see everyone walking around looking like a supermodel 24/7? Working in fashion as a stylist for years I can say that each of those girls is equally as paranoid about their body image. I say to them…when you go to the gym what do you see…do you look at everyone and judge them? Or are you, like them, looking at your own body and worrying about yourself?! That's why many others do not notice that we have scoliosis. When I meet someone I am thinking about their positive features, great eyes or a lovely smile, and so I realise other people think that too.

That mindset has really helped me to overcome how I feel mentally about my spine and I use my experience to encourage younger people going through the same anxiety to be positive about how they look.

Raising awareness of scoliosis has become my mission and my book is available on Amazon.

I have also written The Scoliosis and Spinal Fusion CPD Course (8 points) endorsed by CIMSPA & YMCA. This course is for physiotherapists, exercise professionals, parents, carers and anyone with scoliosis.

For further details please go to:
https://www.scoliosishandbook.com/book-courses

© caroline freedman

Instagram @scoliosishandbook

www.scoliosishandbook.com

Jenny's Story and Progress

This is the story of my Scoliosis and the eventual decision to undertake Spinal Fusion with Implementation – the operation which corrects scoliosis.

My journey started over twelve years ago when I was diagnosed with having Scoliosis. I decided that I would like my condition treated by a Scoliosis/Complex Spines Consultant, so I made contact with the Scoliosis Society in London for their advice, and they very kindly sent me a list of Scoliosis Consultants, and I was very fortunate that there was someone with this expertise at Salford Royal Hospital, which is only 15 miles from where I live.

For 12 years my condition was monitored, and in January 2011, with a Cobb Angle of 44 degrees, spinal fusion surgery was discussed, and finally agreed. I was informed of all the risks and benefits, and between January and September 2011 I underwent a number of tests, including MRI scans, x-rays, bone density x-rays (I also have osteoporosis), blood tests, ECG, etc.

Spinal surgery is an extremely risky operation and must **not** be undertaken lightly. I was informed that there is a high risk of paralysis if the spinal cord is damaged during the operation, pneumonia and chest infections, and DVT is also possible, so this is a decision that must be made very carefully.

On the 20th September, 2011, at the age of 60, I was admitted into Salford Royal Hospital for my operation. I was in the operating theatre for about 10 hours and in the HDU for about 18 hours (I don't remember much about this at all), and then I was moved to the Spinal Ward where I stayed (in a single bedded room) for 11 days. My care at the hospital was second to none – all the staff were excellent, treating me with dignity and respect.

I had expected to have 7 or 8 vertebra fused together, but afterwards I was told that my Consultant had put 22 screws and 2 titanium rods down the whole of my spine (see photo of my x-ray). Apparently, my consultant had originally planned to

119

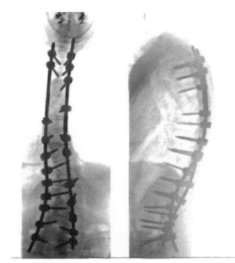

do this operation over two stages – the first in September and the second operation some time later – but it seems that whilst I was on the operating table, he decided to do the whole lot at one go. For this I am extremely grateful – I am not sure if I would want to go through all that again!

Before I was allowed to leave the hospital, I was fitted with a full body brace (similar to a Boston Brace) and was instructed to wear it during the day for the next three months. This garment looks like something that Lady Gaga might wear! I still wear this brace in the car and when out walking (mainly for protection).

Many important factors require consideration when considering spinal surgery, and these are:

- The Consultant **MUST** specialise in scoliosis and complex spines – this for me was extremely important. Spinal surgery has a lot of risks attached to it, so it is important that the Consultant and his team are specialists in this field.
- The patient must understand that he/she will feel quite unwell for several months, and I didn't actually start to feel better until about eight/ten weeks after surgery.
- I also didn't realise how difficult it would be to get the pain medication right. In the hospital I was given liquid morphine (oramorph) which was administered by a syringe, was quite pleasant to take, but relieved the pain very quickly. Once discharged from hospital, with my medical care handed back to my GP, I was only prescribed oramorph one more time due to the fact that oramorph is a 'controlled drug' and highly addictive. This is when the

difficulty started. My GP then prescribed Tramadol as a pain relief. Tramadol is a synthetic narcotic drug and oftener used for post-operative pain, but unfortunately can have a number of bad side effects. It made me very dizzy and tired, but even worst was horrendous hallucinations it gave me, and at this point I decided not to take it anymore. I was then prescribed Dihydracodeine, which is also a synthetic narcotic drug (although not as strong as Tramadol). I decided to take this tablet only at bed time and to take Paracetamol during the day. The side effects of Dihydracodeine were that it made me very itchy and feel nauseous in the morning, which passed after about half an hour. Both these drugs are addictive and GPs will not usually prescribe them for too long. I found that I could not just 'stop' taking Dihydracodeine - I had to reduce it bit by bit over a six month period, until I was just taking an eighth of a tablet each night.

My back still aches a little during the evenings, or when sitting for long periods of time, but I imagine that this is quite normal. Before my operation I was literally living on pain killers, but now I am pleased to say that I only take the occasional Paracetamol. The intense pain that I had before surgery is no longer there. I had been told by my Consultant that I had to give him 'a year of my life', and I was more than happy to do that.

During the early months I tried to go out each day (weather permitting) with my husband and daughter. I started off in a wheelchair, then I progressed to using a walking stick, and after three or four months I found I did not need the walking stick – but even now I still prefer to 'link' an arm when I am out walking. I feel I am still making progress every day.

Recovery from scoliosis surgery is a long process, and even after several years, patients can still feel tired at the end of the day.

I went back to work in March 2012 – initially shorter days, but in August 2012 I decided to go back full time. I do get days when I feel tired and my back aches, but it is so much better now – and it is so wonderful that I don't have that excruciating pain any more.

After my operation I had to go back to the hospital for a one month, three month and six month check-ups, and I finally saw my Consultant again in March 2013, when he discharged me. I was told, however, that if I should have any problems I could go back and see him again – which I find comforting to know.

My grateful thanks must go to my consultant, who has monitored my scoliosis condition for many years, and for 'taking my pain away'

As a Christian, I found great comfort and strength from knowing that I was in the prayers and thoughts of many people, including 'prayer chains' around the country.

In particularly, I am extremely grateful to my husband and daughter for their unfailing love and care, and for looking after me so well – especially during the difficult early months – thank you both so much.

Paula

When I was 13, I had a brace fitted, plaster cast from my neck to my waist, they cut a hole in the front and one in the back, I was given a roll of vest to wear under it…over my head and pushed through the holes to hang out the bottom.

I had a metal rod with a slight bend on the end to help push it down/through. I also pulled the paint off it and used it as a back scratcher, causing cuts and sores so it was confiscated!

I was put onto a rack, neck pulled back while they wrapped the cold plaster around me, they stretched me about 2 inches, I then spent around a week in hospital using a dryer tunnel to dry the plaster, they turned me every few hours to dry it all, I was sick every time I laid on my stomach. 😫

I had this in for 6 months at a time, they took it off, gave me a bath and repeated it on the same day…awful and scary time of my life…hated it.

It took a few people to wash my hair at home, laying me on 4 chairs, one holding my feet as I was too heavy, one holding a towel around my neck and the other washing my hair.

I had to lay on my back in bed and someone had to get me up each morning.

I couldn't take part in PE at school, and people took the Mickey out of me, calling me names etc.

After two years of that they gave me a plastic and metal brace to wear, I had to get in and out of it with a screwdriver, wear it all day and night, and just took it off to bath.

Very uncomfortable.

This lasted until I was 18 then they said my bones had stopped growing so just do exercises as my spine wouldn't get any worse from then.

I led a fairly normal life for a while until I was 25 and it all went downhill then, back aches led to other things.

I had to give up physical jobs because it hurt, I worked as a carer.

I'm now 54 and classed as disabled with a blue badge, mobility scooter as can't walk far, sticks, can't work and on benefits and taking many pills daily, they said a few years back they won't operate as I'm too old, maybe they should have done it when I was younger!

I have different pains all over my body but they say just keep taking the pills, the spinal consultant signed me off and I just see the GP now and then.

I feel it depends on your postcode to the care and attention you need and get so I've resorted to looking after myself.- Paula

If you think you or your child has Scoliosis, you will need to see a GP. they will be able to check to see if you or your child have it. If the GP suspects it is Scoliosis then they will send you to a Scoliosis/spinal specialist. One way to check yourself is to check for uneven hips or waist.

There are three types of Scoliosis which are idiopathic, congenital and neuromuscular.

Idiopathic Scoliosis is the most common out of the three. This basically means that the cause of it is known, or that no single factor contributes to the development.

Signs of Scoliosis include

A curved spine which is visible.

Leaning to one side.

Uneven shoulders.

One shoulder or hip sticking out on one side.

Clothes not fitting well. If you have one shoulder lower or higher than the other then this could mean that t-shirts etc could not fit around the shoulders properly.

Scoliosis can cause back pain; this is generally more common in adults but doesn't mean to say that children don't get the pain.

When you see the GP, they will examine the spine, if from that they think that it's possibly scoliosis then you will be referred to have a X ray done and you'll be referred to s Spinal/scoliosis specialist The X Ray is to see how much the spine is curved and to see how severe it is. If the X ray concludes that you do have scoliosis then a specialist will then discuss your treatment options. The options that you get given will depend on how severe and what the degree of your curve is. Also, age may be dependent on what choices you get. If you're younger they may choose to watch and wait, or try bracing. If you're older then they may decide that as you're a certain age then it would be best not to do anything as big as surgery.

If your curve degree is past a certain number then sometimes surgery may be an option but this depends.

The treatment that is an option or the best choice for you will depend on a range of things. This could be things such as age, how severe your curve is, pain, if it'll get worse over time and there could be other factors which fit into this too. If you have any questions about any of the options that the specialist gives you then it would be a good idea to ask them while you're there, and if you think that an option that you've looked into could be possible.

They are the best people to ask and would be able to explain why these options you got given are best for you and why others wouldn't be best, and why it wouldn't be in your best interest to be able to do it. Though some specialists may say they won't do it and others may say different, sometimes this is why some people get second or third options if they are 100% with the first specialists' choice of treatment choices.

People often think that everyone who has scoliosis generally has some form of treatment such as bracing, surgery, and given exercises just to list a few. But surprisingly not many people actually need any treatment for their Scoliosis. Also along with this not many people actually need to have surgery for it, it's only a small number of people who actually do. This could be the fact it could make them worse, the curve isn't bad enough, it wont get worse, other treatments work just to name a few reasons. Many people think as soon as they hear scoliosis it means they will instantly need an operation which isn't always the case. Most people are lucky and are able to not need it. Just that the small number of people who do need the operation.

Babies and toddlers generally may not need any treatment as their curve may be able to improve over time. But this doesn't mean to say they won't. Depending on how their curve is, it may be just a watch and wait or they may want to do something. But it all depends on how their spine is and if it's likely to improve. It will be down to the specialist who you see who will decide the best way forward for them, and it's always best to ask any questions if you have any. Even though treatment may not be needed, it might get mentioned that they get a cast or brace fitted, this is done to try and stop the curve progressing or getting worse while they are still growing.

In some cases, an operation may need to be done to be able to control the growth of the spine, until it would be possible to be able to do another one to be able to strengthen the spine when they stop growing.

In adults they will possibly need treatment to try and relive the pain that they are in such as painkillers. You may get referred to a pain clinic who will be able to advise you on what to take, what to do to relieve pain, and may be able to give you stronger painkillers if you need it. You may be offered spinal injections and surgery may be a possibility but can't always guarantee that it will relieve the pain.

The cause of most childhood Scoliosis is unknown and no known cause to why they have it.

There are cases when family members have it, but in some families only one person has it. So it's a 50/50 on if it can be genetic or not, but if a family member has it then there is that risk that they could potentially pass it on if they have children, but this isn't always the case.

Scoliosis is a sideways curve, generally can be a C or S shape.

With Scoliosis most cases are considered as mild, but in children as they haven't stopped growing there is a chance that it could get worse as they are growing.

Scoliosis is a progressive condition which means that it will tend to get worse with age.

This doesn't mean though it will have increased the degree on your curve, over a number of years.

Scoliosis won't go away unfortunately, it's basically an incurable and progressive condition so it won't go away or be able to fix itself without any form of treatment. This is why if you suspect you or your child has Scoliosis then you need to see your GP as its best to get it looked at sooner rather than later. This will help with treatment plans if it is definitely Scoliosis.

Some adults who have scoliosis have either had it since birth, childhood or teenagers but isnt always the case, as you can get it at any age. Over time it is possible that the curve can grow.

There's also another form of scoliosis that can start in adulthood. As you get older the wear and tear can damage the bones and the joints in your spine. The disks which sit between them will begin to start breaking down. When this happens the disks will lose height and start to tilt. This will cause your spine to curve.

Often in adults the first spine of possible scoliosis will be back pain. The pain may be from possible bone damage in the back, not just scoliosis itself. As your spine curves it can put pressure onto the nearby nerves, and can cause symptoms such as weakness and numbness.

Scoliosis in adults can cause symptoms such as

Uneven shoulders and/or hips

Bump in the lower back numbness, weakness or pain in the legs.

Trouble walking.

Having trouble standing up straight

Tired feeling

Shortness of breath

Loss of height

Bone spurs which are bone bumps in the joints of the spine from bone and joint damage.

Feeling full quickly is because your spine is putting pressure on your tummy.

Symptoms in children

Their shoulders are two different heights

Their head doesn't look centred with the rest of their body

One hip is higher than the other, or sticks out

The ribs are pushed out

When the child stands straight, their arms don't hang straight down their body

When they bend forward the two sides of their back are at different heights.

Especially in children, these changes can affect their self esteem. This is because they may not like the way they look, or their back. This could make them feel like "they aren't normal" as they don't look like their friends. Especially when and can be made worse by when others stare at them.

Someone was asked to describe how scoliosis pain felt. Their answer was "it feels like a stiffness and tightness in my lower back."

While this is most common within adults, this can also be a common scoliosis related problem. As the body tries to adjust to the abnormal spine curvature, muscles and ligaments can be stretched and strained.

If scoliosis is left untreated it is possible that the curve can go to more than 90 degrees after growth, can cause severe health problems and possibly other factors. So sometimes surgery maybe a choice for you if they think they will need to intervene that way, if other treatment options won't work.

Scoliosis in adults can occur for a number of reasons. These could be things such as genetics, uneven pelvic position, past spinal or joint surgeries, knee or foot distortions or even head injuries.

Some curves are more severe than others. If you have moderate or severe cases it may have to be corrected by bracing and/or surgery. Depending on your case you may have one or the other, or you may have to have both. This will be depending on what your specialist decides which would be the best treatment for you to do.

There is a difference between a typical spine and one with scoliosis. With a typical spine is that the former can move side to side. Example is when you walk your spine will bend and will rotate from left and right, and revert back to the centre. But those who have scoliosis can prove difficult as moving in one direction due to the curve in the spine.

Schroth exercises are scoliosis specific due to the aim of trying to help the posture and pain. This is to teach patients to try and maintain their posture, if possible, in their daily living activities.

These target strength training for the abdominal, back and leg muscles.

A study taken in the USA showed that the patients who used the Schroth exercises made improvements in self image, back muscle and pain level.

Certain exercises may be given to you by a physiotherapist to help with specific structural differences. But this is not a means for treatment. Treatment for moderate to severe cases may involve surgery.

Generally mild scoliosis will not require any significant medical attention, and isn't visible to the eyes as other posture disorders.

Mild scoliosis is generally the term which is used to describe scoliosis where the cobb angle of curvature of the spine is less than 20 degrees. Mild scoliosis is also the most responsive to exercise treatment.

Moderate scoliosis may be treated with exercise, but depending on your options a brace in which you would get fitted by the hospital generally and referred for by the specialist may be recommended. This is depending on what your specialist will work best for you. The moderate type may also develop into the more severe scoliosis, defined as a spine curvature between 40 and 45 degrees.

Severe scoliosis will usually will need to be treated by having spinal surgery to correct it.

Managing Scoliosis
Mild -
Often can be managed with exercise, medical observation, scoliosis specific physiotherapy and possible chiropractic treatment. For some with scoliosis, yoga or Pilates is also recommended to decrease pain level and increase flexibility.

Moderate
Often involves some kind of bracing to stop the spine curving any further.
Depending on the curve of the spine, the specialist might suggest increased medical observation or other treatment methods which may be helpful.

Once the spine reaches a certain curvature and the person reaches a certain age, Surgery comes the most recommended treatment option. Surgery to correct scoliosis can take several forms and depends on a variety of factors which include
The way your spine is shaped
How tall you are
Whether or not parts of your body have been severely impaired by the growth of the spine.

What is a scoliosis brace?

A scoliosis brace is worn around the torso that can help prevent the curve from getting any worse. It can also make it less likely for you to need surgery in the future when the bone growth has stopped.

A brace is the only available treatment in which can potentially slow the progression of the curve in a child or adolescent whose bones are still growing. Bracing won't work if bone growth has stopped.

Different types of bracing

A brace which goes from your thoracic spine (upper back) to your sacral spine (buttocks) is called a thoracic-lumbar-sacral orthosis (TLSO).It covers your body from your armpits to your hips. It's the most common type of brace.

Some braces are worn full time and some which are just worn when you're sleeping.

Milwaukee brace

This was the original brace, this is called CTLSO. It has a metal superstructure and is very noticeable, because it's worn on the outside of clothing rather than underneath. Because of its size, bulk and its appearance it's not a brace which is commonly used much anymore.

Boston Brace

This is the one in which is more commonly being used when bracing is possibly needed. It's a TLSO. It fits like a jacket, and goes from your armpits to your hips. It's made of lightweight plastic, it hasn't got a superstructure, so it isn't really noticed. Especially as this brace goes underneath clothing. A prefabricated brace is customised to your body and spinal curve. You may need help taking it on and off as it closes at the back.

Wilmington brace

This is similar to the Boston brace. It's made out of the same material but is closed at the front instead of the back. It's made by using a plaster mould of your torso.

Night time bracing

Charleston bending brace

This is the most prescribed night time brace, this is a TLSO. It's customised to fit your curve and body. It puts strong pressure on the spine, bending it past the midline of your back. The overcorrection is only possible when you're lying down.

How effective is bracing?
Bracing has been used for over 450 years for treating scoliosis. Even after that many years there are still questions about its effectiveness.
Bracing can only stop or slow down the progression of the curve. They can't get rid of it, nor can it straighten the spine.

Bracing won't work if it's not worn for the length of time needed or isn't being worn correctly.
If the brace isn't fitting properly then you need to be re-seen to get it fixed as you may need to have a new one fitted.

What other treatments are there for scoliosis?

How your scoliosis is managed depends on:
How mature your bones are. If the bones are still growing then it's likely that a brace may be recommended.

Where the spine is curved
Curves in the upper back tend to get worse more often than in other areas.
How severe the curve is
Generally bracing is only used for curves between 25 and 40 degrees. Curves over 40 are often treated with surgery.

Observation
If your curve is mild then the specialist may want to just wait and see what happens, rather than treat it. If the curve starts to get worse then treatment may be recommended.

Children may see the specialist every 4-6 months until they are teens. Unless things are getting worse than adults are usually followed with an X ray every 5 years.

Surgery
Braces can only slow the progression down. Surgery can potentially fix the curve in addition to stopping it getting any worse.

Surgery recommendations are based on:

Age

Previous treatment

How severe the curve is

Surgery is recommended when
The curve is larger than 40 degrees and in a child who is progressing.

A surgical procedure that needs to be revised when they are an adult.

The curve is 50 degrees or higher and there are signs of nerve damage, indicating spinal stenosis.

Most cases surgery involves fusing spinal segments (vertebrae) together after straightening the spine with solid metal rods.

Tia Deacon

Photos from the charity fundraiser I did 2018/19

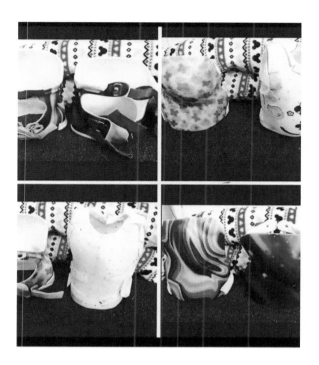

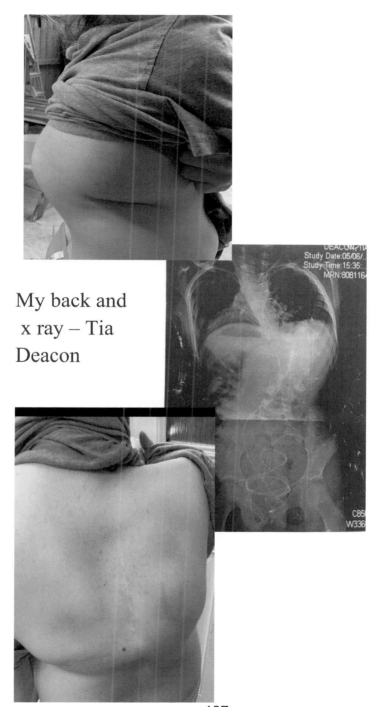

My back and
x ray – Tia
Deacon

Scoliosis Campaign Fund

When raising for SCF you are helping 2 charities. Any money raised will be split between the two.

SAUK = www.sauk.org.uk
BSRF = www.bsrf.co.uk

Join as a member and other emails will be written on paper or can be found on their sites.

In around 8 in every cases the cause of Scoliosis in unknown.

It can affect anyone at any age but most often in ages 10-15.

Signs of Scoliosis include
A visably curved spine, leaning to one side, uneven shoulders, one shoulder or hip sticking out, the ribs sticking out on one side and clothes not fitting well

Scoliosis Association UK

Your money helps:

Run a nationwide support network of members and volunteers.

Run a helpline where people can call or email SAUK for support, advice or just someone to talk to.

Produces peer-reviewed health information and a magazine called backbone.

Travel across the UK to hold meetings

Keeps up to date list of Scoliosis specialists allowing people with Scoliosis to find where to go for best available treatment.

Campaigns for better understanding of the condition and to spread awareness.

half money raised will go towards British Scoliosis research foundation.

You can help also by fundraising, spreading awareness on social media, take part in Scoliosis international day, buy SAUK merchandise from their shop, Join as a member or volunteer to support and advise those with Scoliosis

Printed in Great Britain
by Amazon

83858953R00078